Three Sheets

DRINKING MADE EASY!
6 CONTINENTS, 15 COUNTRIES,
190 DRINKS, AND 1 MEAN HANGOVER!

Three Sheets

Zane Lamprey

Villard
New York

This book is for the fans. Without you I'd just be a drunk guy with a monkey . . .

Contents

THREE SHEETS TO THE WIND: 1. An old nautical phrase that referred not to the sails on a ship, but to the ropes that held the sails in place. When all three sheets were not tied down, the sails would flap in the wind and the boat would wobble as it left the harbor. 2. To be inebriated to the point that you wobble when you walk, like a ship without its sheets secured. 3. A book and television show about drinking.

How to Use This Book

There are two types of tourists: the kind that plan their vacation out and the kind that fly by the seat of their pants. If you're the former, your last overseas vacation probably consisted of zipping about, hitting as many monuments, museums, and scenic overlooks as you could fit into your typed-out itinerary. You probably picked up a guidebook with a foldout map and had a preplanned schedule to make sure you made the most of each day. If you're the latter, you probably spent a few minutes on the Internet, looking at pretty pictures of where you were going. You probably thought "whatever happens, happens." Then you realized that all of the hotels were booked, so you fell asleep in the train station, and when you woke up someone handed you a euro because they thought you were homeless—which you essentially were.

This book is exactly what both kinds of travelers need. But instead of focusing on the typical tourist traps, it will tell you how to have a unique experience in whatever country you visit. Instead of statues of dictators, go in search of the elusive Zubrówka, illegal in America but very popular in Poland. Instead of a tour bus to the middle of the spring break area of Mexico, take a Tequila Train to the heart of tequila-making country. In my search for the best places to drink, and the best things in the world to drink, I've tasted the finest champagnes and cognacs in their respective regions in France and learned from master vintners about how they are made. I've knocked back 100-proof kaoliang infused with snake blood in Taipei and I've sipped Scotch that will set you back a cool ten thousand dollars a bottle in Scotland. I've tried a dozen varieties of vodka in Poland, visited a bar in Belgium that serves more than two thousand beers, and traced the path of the Malbec grape from France to Argentina. I met some really incredible people along the way. I learned some fascinating things about the world—and the way the world drinks. And now you can share in the reward of all of my "hard work."

Spend a hundred dollars on a bus tour and you'll see the land and learn about its history. Spend a hundred in a pub buying a few rounds and you'll learn about the people who *made* the land and who *live* the history.

Sure, statues and monuments that pay homage to a country's wars, plagues, and famines say a lot about the people who live there. And you can often find a fine adventure if you just aimlessly bumble about and hope for the best. But the best way to learn about the people who live in a particular place is not by observing their history, or learning about the people who died off years ago, but by talking with the people who live there now. And in my experience, nothing works better as a social lubricant and as a way to get people to open up than buying a round. You'll get some great advice about where the locals eat and drink, will probably get invited to hang out with them again, and will most likely make some friends for life. Not bad for the price of a drink.

The Book

This isn't a traditional guidebook. This book will paint a picture of what drinking in a country or region is like and hopefully inspire you to journey to some of the amazing places that I've had the privilege to visit. I'll speak of specific locations and customs, but don't expect to see any detailed maps, hotel recommendations, or tips on how to get around town. There are other books out there for that. What I can promise is to give you some really good reasons to go to some really cool places and to have a few libations while you're there.

I'll even buy you one myself: On a trip to Scotland, I was made a member of the Craigellachi Whisky Club at the Quaich Bar in the Craigellachi Hotel of Speyside. I keep a bottle of Glenfiddich 18 in the case. If you stop by the bar, mention that you're a friend of mine and help yourself to a nip from my bottle.

Why do I get to spend so much time wearing down my passport and get paid for something that everyone else would pay to do? For the past few years, I have hosted a television show, *Three Sheets,* which has sent me to locations across the globe to engage in foreign drinking customs and befriend the people who partake in them. My "job" has taken me to more than fifty countries, where I have visited countless watering holes, drunk innumerable libations, and had my share of debilitating hangovers. I've traveled around the world, drinking...so you don't have to. The most common question I'm asked is "What's your favorite drink?" My response is "Usually, the drink that I'm drinking." When you're enjoying someone's drink of choice, in the place where it was developed, with the people who revere it, it's difficult to desire anything else at that moment. When someone is so passionate about a beverage, it's difficult to not be affected.

I have one of the best jobs in the world, not only because I am gainfully employed doing something that most people consider a leisure-time activity, but also because when I do it, I get a truly authentic experience from the countries that I visit.

Cast of Characters

Steve McKenna

Throughout this book and while shooting *Three Sheets*, I often make references to my buddy Steve McKenna. He's one of my closest friends and one of the nicest guys you'd ever meet. However, when Steve drinks, he gets a little nutty. When he hits his threshold of drinks, he becomes a gremlin. It's not unlike Dr. Jekyll and Mr. Hyde, although Steve doesn't hold any postgraduate degrees, so he's more like Mr. Jekyll and Mr. Hyde. His Mr. Jekyll is a guy who would wake up at 5 A.M. to drive you to the airport, would help you move, and would return your car washed and full of gas if he were to borrow it. His Mr. Hyde would drink until 5 A.M., move you to tears, and throw up in your car after having very bad gas in it. His name, completely my doing, has become synonymous with high levels of intoxication. You're buzzed if you get the courage to talk to someone that you wouldn't talk to when you're sober. You're drunk if you try to kiss someone that you wouldn't talk to when you're sober. And you're "Steve McKenna'd" if you lick the face of someone you wouldn't talk to sober. There are several Steve McKenna references in this book. Now you'll know who and what I'm referring to . . .

Pleepleus

Pleepleus is the name of the stuffed toy monkey that I bring along with me on my travels. He's been with me in every episode, except for when I left him in a beer bath in the Czech Republic, or when I forgot him completely in Jamaica and Costa Rica. He was origi-nally hidden in the show, as part of the drinking game that people play when they watch *Three Sheets* on TV, but now Pleepleus occasion-ally upstages me.

Jim-the-Cop

Jim-the-Cop is another buddy of mine. He was a cop on Long Island, New York, until he got in-jured on the job and had to re-tire (it was a back injury, nothing cool like being shot in the leg). So he found ample time to tag along with me for a couple of episodes. The first time he joined me was in Puerto Rico. I challenged him and the owner of Nono's to a chugging contest, to see who could down a glass of beer the fastest. I came in first, and Jim came in last. A few months later we were in New York City shooting an episode at Lederhosen, a great German bar in

Greenwich Village. I wanted to give Jim a chance to vindicate himself, so I organized another chugging contest. What was only revealed later was that Jim was advised by his brother to "spill a little beer down his shirt" so he could empty the glass more quickly. Not only did he lose, but he ended up with a spill down his shirt. That day a new expression was born. Now, whenever someone spills a drink, it's said that they "Jim-the-Cop'd."

Drink!

While shooting the first episode of *Three Sheets*, I thought it would make sense to also make the show a drinking game. A lot of other shows have become drinking games after the fact, such as *M*A*S*H* and *Cheers*. You gotta drink when Klinger shows up in women's clothing or when Cliff Claven gives a "little-known fact." But those games were created after the shows were made, and didn't always work. I wanted to create a game so people watching could drink along with me. Why just *watch* a party on TV when you can party along? The game became a big hit.

Think of the book as an international pub crawl. You don't have to buy a round-the-world ticket and tackle each chapter while you're physically in the region we're discussing. But if you have the means to, I highly recommend it. The alternative way to read this book is to drink along. *Three Sheets* was the first television show to be deliberately made as a drinking game. So why shouldn't *Three Sheets* the book follow suit? Not drinking along would be like reading about some great art in a book with no pictures. That's crazy talk! So, the rules for the drinking game, if you care to partake, are as follows: Whenever you read the words *drink*, *drank*, or *drunk*, take a sip. Therefore, if you're playing along, you just took three. Whenever I talk about Steve McKenna, you have to say "Oh, boy . . ." out loud and take a sip. And whenever you see Pleepleus hiding on a page, tap him on the head and take a sip! Try not to get Steve McKenna'd and be careful not to Jim-the-Cop!

Mind Your Manners

The world of booze has a different set of borders than the geopolitical world represented on a globe, and this book is organized accordingly. Sometimes the chapters are focused on a country, but other times it's a region, and sometimes it's a specific city. A weekend in Las Vegas is not what you'd call a typical American experience. Tequila, Mexico, is a vastly different place from Mexico City. And if you go to Champagne, you are talking about a unique region in its own right, and to just refer to it as France would be . . . well . . . a faux pas.

Learn by Doing

When you're done with this book you should be able to confidently discuss the differences between whisky and whiskey, tequila and mescal, and champagne and sparkling wines. You'll know the difference between ales and lagers. And you will have the ability to intelligently order from the sake menu in a Japanese restaurant based on more than just the prices.

Having your own experiences are key in understanding and appreciating various libations. I can only convey so much. Using words to describe flavor is like trying to describe a color. All I can do is compare it to things you already know. So expand your palate, and your liquor cabinet, and taste what I'm saying. Of course, Scotch, tequila, and champagne will be easier for you to get your hands on than kaoliang infused with snake blood, a fifty-year-old Scotch, or New

Zealand moonshine, but just do your best. Knowledge without experience seems like a waste, like that Nuclear Arms and Weapons Control class I took in college (I wish I were joking—but my roommate's fraternity brother had the tests). What do I care about radioactive isotopes if I can't get my hands on some?! And shouldn't someone in the government be concerned that I aced the class?

By the time you're done with the book, you won't just be able to explain why different whiskies have different flavor qualities, but you'll really appreciate the difference a little spring water, peat moss, wood barrels, and roasted barley can make.

The Hangover Remedy Rating System

In the following pages, you'll find information about everything from guavaberries to fermented sorghum: what it is, how it's made, its cultural significance, and how to drink it. So as you go through the Ireland chapter grab a Guinness, pick up a single malt when we get to Scotland, and mix a mojito for St. Martin. And don't worry about overdoing it. Every country that drinks has hangovers, despite what many may claim, and they all have their own attempts at hangover remedies.

If you get into it as much as I do, you too will encounter an occasional rough morning. But fear not, because as I said, every country that has hangovers has a hangover remedy—a *remedy,* not a "cure." If there were some special tea or food out there that cured your hangover, it wouldn't be secret for long. The special "herbal" tea that I had in Jamaica and the *tortas ahogadas* that I had in Mexico helped, but they didn't make me want to hit the town right away. How well did they work? Well...that's very subjective, relative to the previous night. So, I'll rate them one sheet, two sheets, or three sheets. A hangover remedy that gets a one-sheet rating would do the trick if you only had a few beers the night before. Two sheets is for the morning after you had more than a few but you still remember how you got home. A remedy that's three sheets is effective for even the surliest hangovers—the ones that usually linger until well into the next evening. The ones Steve McKenna complains about. Drink!

Six Continents and Counting

As soon as I'm invited to have a drink in Antarctica, I'm there. Until then, I'm pleased to have gotten tipsy with the locals in North America, South America, Europe, Africa, Asia, and Oceania. We're starting our tour in Europe because that's where so many of the drinks that we encounter in the other continents have their roots. Colonialism not only creates empires, it exports and imports ideas of how to kick back and have a drink. So make a run to your local liquor store, get comfortable, and get ready to drink your way around the world . . .

Three Sheets

Europe

Our pub crawl begins across the Atlantic on a continent long renowned for storied past, incredible culture, and inbred monarchies. Lucky for us, culture goes beyond the ghosts of civilizations past and extends to one of my own favorite pastimes—indulging in its spirits. The continent's history is so long and so entrenched that there's been plenty of time for people to get together and figure out how to turn the stuff they eat into stuff they can drink. Especially since, back in the days before Evian, it was often safer to drink the booze than it was to drink the water.

We'll visit the birthplace of whiskey, the only region in the world where *real* champagne is made, and the country where beer is so revered, it's made by holy men. Then we'll head east to the Vodka Belt and find out what bison have to do with booze, why people put gold into liquor, and what the vodka-to-people ratio for a Polish wedding is (okay, I'll tell you: one bottle to each person).

Europe is not only beautiful, it's delicious. And if done right, it can get you very, very tipsy.

Chapter 1

Ireland

Latitude: 53°00' N

Longitude: 8°00' W

What they call it: Éire

What they speak: English, Irish (Gaelic)

How to say cheers: *Sláinte!* (Health!)

Hangover remedy: Irish coffee

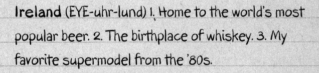

Ireland (EYE-uhr-lund) 1. Home to the world's most popular beer. 2. The birthplace of whiskey. 3. My favorite supermodel from the '80s.

While the Irish may not be able to take credit for inventing intoxication, their contributions to the field have been numerous. And the world has been paying attention. Most Americans over the age of twenty-one can name Ireland's most popular beer,[1] whiskey,[2] and the city that they both originated in,[3] and St. Patrick's Day has become an excuse for Irish and non-Irish alike to drink until they speak in limericks. Which makes sense. I mean, even their coffee has alcohol in it.

Just a Pint, Please. Okay, Maybe Two...or Four

On the east coast of Ireland, Dublin, the country's capital, has over one thousand registered pubs. There are so many drinking establishments that Irish author James Joyce, in his novel *Ulysses*, proposed that "a good puzzle would be to cross Dublin without passing a pub." It still strikes natives as an impossible task—so much so that a radio station had a competition to see who could come up with a walking

[1] Guinness.
[2] Jameson.
[3] Dublin.

route that would take them from one side of the city to the other without passing a pub. For months, there was no winner. Finally someone offered a logical solution. "When I come to a pub, I don't pass it," he said. "I stop for a pint, and then carry on."

The bronze medal for beers in Ireland goes to Smithwick's (pronounced "Shmid-icks"), a "red ale" that was originally produced at St. Francis Abbey Brewery in Kilkenny, which is Ireland's oldest operating brewery. It was founded by John Smithwick in 1710 but was sold to Guinness in 1965. (Along with much of the distilled and brewed world, they're both owned by Diageo.) Today it is produced in Kilkenny and in Dundalk. Smithwick's is Ireland's third-best-selling beer but is often considered a favorite among locals.

Murphy's, our silver medal winner, has been made in Cork, in the south of Ireland, since 1856. It's considered a "dry stout," which is similar to Guinness, but has a slightly lighter and drier taste. Murphy's contains nitrogen, along with carbon dioxide, to give it its creamy consistency (like Guinness). It is the favored beer in the south of Ireland, and the second most popular beer overall.

And the gold medal winner for the most popular beer in Ireland goes to . . . (as if you didn't know) Guinness.

Guinness for Strength

The green isle is renowned as the birthplace of Yeats, Joyce, Bono—and Guinness. Guinness is based on a porter style of beer that was popular in London in the early 1700s. Made from roasted, malted barley, hops, yeast, and water, it's classified as a "dry stout." Although it's often called "black," the manufacturer insists that when held up to the light, it's actually a dark ruby. I've never had the patience to find out. If I hold a Guinness up to anything, it's going to be my mouth. The taste, if you haven't yet had the pleasure, is beer meets rich and creamy with hints of coffee and chocolate, which it gets from the heavily roasted, malted barley. While it's not as heavy-tasting as it sounds, it's often called a "meal in a glass" because of all the vitamins it contains.

Back in 1759, Arthur Guinness purchased Dublin's St. James Brewery. Since his family name already carried some weight around town, he convinced the city to lease him the property for forty-five pounds (about sixty dollars) a year. That was a pretty good deal, but to make it even sweeter, that lease isn't set to increase until the year 10,759. You read that correctly: He got a nine-thousand-year lease!

In Ireland, if you've just given blood or given birth, you might expect to be given a pint of Guinness (for strength).

Today, Guinness is one of the most successful beer brands in the world, brewed in 51 countries and sold in 150. Every day, over 10 million glasses of the "dark stuff" are enjoyed around the planet, and 1.8 billion pints are sold every year.

The brand is known not just for its rich brew, but also for some very successful advertising campaigns. The most memorable ads were created by artist John Gilroy in the 1930s. Playing up the claim that the beer's vitamin content makes it healthy, the posters announced "Guinness Makes You Strong," "Guinness for Strength," and on a poster featuring frothy, smiling mugs of the brew, simply "Guinness Is Good for You." Today that wouldn't fly. Even in Europe, advertising claims need to be substantiated by significant proof. But those excellent retro posters are still available in the Guinness store at St. James Gate!

Guinness has a rich taste, but despite its creamy consistency, it's actually lower in calories than many light beers. The imperial pints they pour in Ireland are slightly larger than a pint in the United States, but if calculated per ounce, a Guinness is significantly lower in calories than a Budweiser and only slightly higher in calories than a Bud Lite. It also contains fewer calories than a pint of skim milk, a pint of orange juice, or a Banana Berry Jamba Juice. Guinness, it does a body good (um, in moderation).

	Serving Size	Calories per Serving	Calories per Ounce
BUD LITE	16 oz. pint	110	9.2
GUINNESS	20 oz. imperial pint	198	9.9
BUDWEISER	16 oz. pint	145	12.1
ORANGE JUICE	16 oz. pint	200	12.5
SKIM MILK	16 oz. pint	260	16.3
JAMBA JUICE	24 oz. Styrofoam cup	450	18.8

The International Guinness Pub Crawl Challenge

When I was in Dublin, I did like the natives do: When I passed a pub, I went in to check it out. One of my favorites is a place called Mulligan's. It was there that I decided Guinness truly does taste better in Ireland than anywhere else. To me, it was creamier, smoother, and without the bitter aftertaste that it sometimes has in the States. According to some, this may be because the water in Ireland is "softer" than our water, which is treated and chlorinated, therefore making it much "harder" and higher in minerals. According to Guinness, they're wrong, primarily because all of the Guinness served in North America is brewed in Ireland.

It tasted fresher to me. But whereas I might be "officially" wrong, I'm not alone. Guinness has heard that claim so many times that they put it to the test. So far, in blind trials, "human test subjects" could not conclusively say that Guinness brewed in Ireland tasted any better than Guinness brewed in other countries. While I won't concede, I will suggest that ambiance makes a big difference in enjoyment, and the experience of having a rich, creamy pint of cold Guinness on a cloudy day in Ireland adds another level of deliciousness.

So I'm going to suggest another trial. Think of it as a scientifically motivated long-distance pub crawl that will net you airline miles and another stamp in your passport: Have a Guinness in the States, have one in Dublin, and then make your own decision.

The Rich Man *Is* the Pour Man

Guinness isn't only creamier than other beers, it's needier. You can't just pour a glass once—you have to pour it twice. Waiting at the bar for my third pint, I wondered if the two-stage pour was clever marketing or a necessary step in its preparation. Guinness says that the added step in the pouring of its beer is required because of the nitrogen content. A typical beer is carbonated with 100 percent carbon dioxide. Most of the CO_2 is released when the beer is poured, which causes a lot of fizziness, but if poured properly, the beer settles quite quickly. Guinness, however, is pressurized with 75 percent nitrogen and only 25 percent carbon dioxide. Therefore, when the pressure is released from Guinness, it creates a much creamier head that is slower to settle, therefore requiring it to be poured in two stages.

How to Properly Pour a Guinness

For the first pour, the glass should be tilted at a 45-degree angle and filled to three-quarter capacity. Then you must wait patiently for the beer to settle, or "cook," before topping it off. Once the surge of bubbles beneath the foam settles, you place the glass under the tap and, instead of pulling, you push the tap, or "back it," away from you. According to Guinness, the finished product should take "roughly" 119.5 seconds to create and should be served at 6 degrees Celcius, or 42.8 degrees Fahrenheit.

Pouring a Guinness "poorly," or in one stage instead of the required two (I plead guilty to one count of each), may result in "frog's eyes." These are bubbles in the foamy head of the pint, which resemble a frog's eyes breaking the surface of a muddy pond. I was three beers in, so I drank my mistakes, not to worry—no beers were wasted in the writing of this chapter. My third mistake was not filling the glass to the very top. According to the bartender, and some concerned patrons looking on, a pint of Guinness isn't complete until the foamy head peeks over the top of the glass (capillary action at work).

In Ireland, pubs close midweek at 11:30 P.M. with a half-hour drink-up time. Friday and Saturday it's 12:30 A.M. closing. Every pub shuts down on Good Friday and Christmas Day. Most nightclubs with a full bar will serve drinks until about 2:30 A.M. Pubs have been smoke-free since 2004.

Because the frothy consistency of the head is so thick, you can make a pattern in the foam while topping off the glass. I've seen it done in the States, where some Irish pubs finish off their pints with a cute little shamrock. But that's like the original Star Wars trilogy—sometimes adding special effects can actually mess with a good thing.

Go West, Young Man

After you've drunk your fill in Dublin, you might make your way away from the murky waters of Dublin's River Liffey and toward the tempestuous, craggy coast of Galway, a city on Ireland's west coast, to see what's happening on the "other side of town." Galway is known for its arts, its festivals, and its harbors. The roads to Galway are surrounded by green fields dotted with sheep; the city center is a green square called Eyre Square or Kennedy Park, which is dotted with, well, people. Almost all of these people have, at least once, stepped foot in the King's Head Pub, where I learned a lot about all the delightful things you can do with Guinness.

I'd Like a Black and Tan. Isn't That *Special?*

When I was in college, where we may have spent more nights at the bars than we did studying, my good buddy Steve McKenna and I frequently enjoyed one of our favorite Guinness concoctions: the black and tan.

A black and tan, as we enjoyed them, consisted of a pint glass filled to about four-fifths with Harp's lager and topped off with Guinness. The Guinness was poured over the back of a spoon, dispersing it so the stout wouldn't mix with the lager. The end result was a tasty and creamy beer that was half black (Guinness), half tan (Harp), and all gooood. (The math doesn't add up because the Guinness is overbearing.)

The black and tan was not a regular offering at the King's Head. But when the bartender heard the recipe, he said that they had something similar, called a "special."

HOW TO MAKE A SPECIAL

Filled a pint glass almost to the top with Smithwick's.

Finish it off with a wee bit of Guinness.

According to the bartender, Guinness is added just to give the lager a creamy head, not to combine the flavors as in a black and tan.

Meet Bailey's. It's Da Bomb!

A popular liquor in Ireland is Baileys Irish Cream, a key ingredient in one of my and Steve's favorite Guinness-based drinks: the Irish Car

---

PROOF VS. PERCENTAGE

To get the "proof" of a bottle of booze, you merely double the percentage of alcohol. A bottle of 90-proof vodka contains 45 percent ethanol alcohol. The term *proof* comes from eighteenth-century Britain. Sailors, to ensure that their rum had not been watered down, tested it by pouring it over gunpowder. If the gunpowder burned, it was "proof" that the rum had not been diluted. Such rum was said to be "100 degrees proof," a strength found to be 57 percent alcohol. Proof was initially figured as following a ratio of 7:4, but then those clever folks in the United States reestablished it as 2:1 (easier math).

Steve McKenna'd: to be inebriated to the point where one loses control over one's actions. If you have to apologize for something that you did while you were under the influence of an alcoholic beverage, you were Steve McKenna'd.

HOW TO MAKE AN IRISH CAR BOMB

IRISH CAR BOMB

Fill half a pint glass with Guinness.

Fill half a shot glass with Jameson Irish whiskey and top that off by "floating in" (pouring it slowly so the liquids do not mix) some Baileys Irish Cream.

Hold the full shot glass just above the pint glass and drop it in the Guinness.

Drink in one fell swoop.

Bomb. Baileys is a delicious blend of Irish whiskey and cream (as well as some other flavorings, such as vanilla, chocolate, and sugar). When it was invented, the creators had trouble preventing the cream and alcohol (which is currently 34 proof) from separating. But through a secret process, the problem was solved and in 1974, Baileys, the world's original cream liqueur, was introduced to the world.

I was curious about whether the Irish Car Bomb was big in Ireland, but I was equally concerned that polling its popularity with the

Date

Sláinte (SLAWN-chuh), meaning "Health" or "To your health!" is the most common toast in Ireland. Another popular Irish toast is "Sláinte mhiaph saoil fada is bás in Eireann," which translates into "Good health, long life, and may you die in Ireland." In the town of Spiddal, however, I was taught an alternative version, which goes, "Sláinte bradán, bod mór, agus bás in Eireann." That one translates into "The health of the salmon, a large penis, and a death in Ireland." Hmm... I'll take the first two and then get the hell outa Ireland!

natives could have some diplomatic ramifications. Later in the night, I checked in with some locals, who were not offended. If you haven't had the pleasure, I highly recommend this drink. It's rich, creamy, and tasty—and almost the equivalent of two shots. So take caution: It's easy to overindulge without knowing it. A few of those and you'll be Steve McKenna'd—guaranteed.

The Water of Life

When in Galway, be sure to visit a town to the north called Spiddal and drink in a pub called Tigh Hughes. What makes the pub, and in fact the entire town, so unique is that they speak primarily Irish there. Irish (we may mistakenly call it Gaelic, but they call it Irish because it's Ireland's form of Gaelic) was the language of Ireland before the

British invasion. When the British propaganda dubbed Irish the "language of peasants," most people adopted English as their primary language. But in Spiddal and many other small towns around Ireland, people still choose to speak the language of their forefathers.

I must admit that I was a little unsure about visiting Tigh Hughes. I had been advised to mind my manners because the locals probably wouldn't take too kindly to outsiders, especially a loud-mouthed Yank. But, as I've since learned, you should never have too many expectations or entirely believe everything you hear.

When I visited, the people at Tigh Hughes were a little closed off at first, although I like to think that they were shy. After I quietly assimilated myself into my surroundings and (perhaps more important) bought a few rounds, I found everyone there to be warm and welcoming. And the "peasants" were anything but; in fact, most of the people I met worked at the local Irish-language television station.

A man at the bar barked something in Irish to the bartender and four shots of whiskey instantly arrived. At this point I was fairly well versed in Ireland's beers, but I was about to get an education in Irish whiskeys and how and why they differ from Scotch, American, and Canadian varieties.

Guy: I'll teach you somethin' about Irish whiskey.
Zane: Okay . . . Why are there four shots?
Guy: Two are fer drinkin', and two are fer talkin' about.

After we threw back our shots, the guy told me that the word *whiskey* is derived from the Irish term *uisce beatha,* which translates to "water of life."

The Irish Invented Whiskey...

There's a popular saying (well, maybe not in Ireland) that the Irish invented whiskey, but the Scottish perfected it. That's a matter of opinion. The truth is a little more complicated. In Ireland, and in the United States, *whiskey* is usually spelled with an *e*. In fact, Ireland actually adopted the *e* to distinguish itself from Scotch whisky, which around 1870 was considered by most of the world to be an inferior product. In Scotland, Wales, Japan, Canada, Germany, and India, they drop the *e* and call it *whisky*. In the United States, if you want Scotch whisky, you have to order a Scotch. If you order "whiskey" in the United States, you'll get a Tennessee whiskey or a bourbon. In Scotland, Scotch is simply called "whisky." Confused? Perfect. Let's continue.

The Irish have single malts, single grains, blended whiskeys, and pure pot still whiskeys. The Scottish, on the other hand, make single

POT STILLS VS. COLUMN STILLS

Distillation is basically a process for separating liquid by means of evaporation and condensation. With a pot still, heat is applied directly to the pot holding the mash, which is the mixture of grains and water that has developed all the delightful enzymes that will help it turn into a good excuse for a party instead of a fermenting mess. This is known as batch distillation—one pot, some heat, and you get a batch of booze. A column still works a little differently, using steam that moves through different levels for a process known as continuous distillation. A column still is sort of like a bunch of pot stills working together. That's the sort of cooperation I can really get behind.

malts, vatted malts, and blends. The Scots often use peat in the roasting process, which makes the whisky taste earthier than Irish whiskey (you'll learn more about this in chapter 3).

Irish Whiskeys

Single malt: 100 percent malted barley that is distilled for your drinking pleasure in a pot still.

Single grain: Distilled in a column still, but usually blended with single malt instead of being sold solo.

Blended whiskey: Grain whiskey blended with single malt.

Pure pot still whiskey: This kind of whiskey is specific to Ireland; it is usually a blend of malted barley and barley that has not been malted; the mixture is then distilled in a pot still.

Across the Atlantic from the great whiskey/whisky debate, you have your Canadian and American varieties. There are countless varieties of whiskey from the United States and Canada. The North American versions might contain some barley, but they are also made with corn and often include other grains, such as wheat and rye (sometimes exclusively, but usually in some combination). American bourbon whiskey is always aged in new American white oak barrels, giving the makers less leeway in terms of spicing up the aging process.

> The largest pot still in the world is in the Old Midleton Distillery in County Cork. It can hold 31,618 gallons of whiskey, enough to inebriate a lot of Irishmen. But nobody uses it anymore, which really just sounds like a great big waste.

My feeling is that in Scotland they make the world's *best* whisky. And in Ireland they make the world's *best* whiskey. That should keep me safe, except against the Canadians and Americans. I'm not worried about the Canadians; they're nice people. And as for the Americans, well, I know a few, so I'll take it up with them personally.

Should you find yourself in the company of die-hard whisky and whiskey fans, you can calm the collective nerves by pointing out what Scotch whisky and Irish whiskey have in common. The Irish and Scotch versions are always distilled from barley, sometimes roasted, sometimes not, sometimes combined in various ratios. Both varieties often make use of wine, bourbon, and even rum barrels that have already been used, which give the makers an opportunity to introduce new and interesting flavor nuances to the aging process.

Once you've done your due diligence, you'll find that the best whiskey/whisky is the one you like the most. My only question is, if Scottish whisky is called "Scotch," shouldn't Irish whiskey be called "Itch"?

John Jameson's family motto, *Sine Metu*, meaning "Without Fear," still appears on every bottle of Jameson Irish whiskey.

Jameson: Distilled in Cork, but Corked in Dublin

The bestselling Irish whiskey in the world is produced by Jameson, which has been making a blended Irish whiskey since the company was founded in Dublin in 1780, when the American Revolution was well under way. Before Prohibition, Jameson *was* the bestselling whiskey in America. Prohibition clearly put a stop to that in 1919, and exports of Jameson to the United States ground to a halt. At least they still had the British market, right? Well, Jameson *was* the most popular whiskey in the British Empire until 1922. After Irish independence, English tariff barriers priced it out of the market. Without overseas demand, all four hundred Irish whiskey brands fell into decline. The future looked bleak for John Jameson & Son and the Irish distillery business.

In a last-ditch effort to keep Irish whiskey alive, in 1966 three distilleries—Jameson, Powers, (which was formed in Dublin in 1791), and Cork Distilleries (from 1825)—joined forces and formed Irish Distillers. Today, Jameson whiskey is distilled in Cork, but vatting still takes place in Dublin. Their strategy was obviously very effective—they have annual sales of over 22 million bottles.

At a U2 concert in Glasgow, Scotland, in 2006, Dublin-born singer Bono supposedly asked the audience for total quiet. He then began slowly clapping his hands. The audience joined in, thinking it was the beginning of a new song. After a few moments, he leaned into the microphone and said, "Every time I clap my hands, a child in Africa dies." To this a man in the front of the crowd said, in a thick Scottish accent, "Well, fuckin' stop doin' it then, ya evil bastard!" I know, it's got nothing to do with drinking, but it's a funny story.

My Coffee Has a Hair in It!

Although Jameson is the most popular and recognizable Irish whiskey outside of Ireland, the most popular brand inside Ireland is Powers Gold Label. The two brands are not rivals but kinsmen, as they are both owned by the Irish Distillers Group, which was bought by Pernod Ricard in 1989.

In my travels, I've found that two of the most common hangover remedies are a cup of java and a little hair of the dog. In Ireland, you're not forced to choose, as the traditional Irish coffee has both coffee and whiskey in it. And although you won't find it at Starbucks (yes, they've invaded Ireland as well), you'll find it just about everywhere else. It is typically made with instant coffee (Ew!), hot water (Duh!), Irish whiskey (Nice!), sugar (Sweet!), and fresh cream (Cool!).

Irish saying: *An rud nach leigheasann im ná uisce beatha níl aon leigheas air.* Translation: What butter or whiskey does not cure cannot be cured.

HOW TO MAKE IRISH COFFEE

Begin by heating up an Irish coffee mug designed specifically for this purpose, with steam or hot water.

Add a scoop or two of freeze-dried coffee crystals.

Fill halfway with hot water.

Add an ounce of whiskey (or more).

Stir in some sugar.

Top with fresh whipped cream.

After drinking your whiskey, sugar, and coffee, be prepared to feel like flying—only to crash back to earth an hour and a half later. The only way to not crash from your booze, sugar, and caffeine rush? Keep drinking! Sláinte!

Remedy rating: *Three out of Three Sheets! You'll feel great, until you get another hangover from the remedy . . .*

Chapter 2

Champagne, France

Latitude: 49°18' N

Longitude: 4°02' E

What they call it: Champagne

What they speak: French

How to say cheers: À votre santé! (To your health!) or Santé!

Hangover remedy: French onion soup

Champagne (sham-PANE) 1. A region in northeast France known to be the birthplace of sparkling wine. 2. A dry, sparkling wine produced in Champagne, France. 3. The color of my grandmother's Buick.

Jay-Z drank Cristal until he boycotted it due to comments from its managing director that he considered racist. He pulled it from his 40/40 clubs and replaced it with Dom Pérignon. "Dom's now the king, and Cristal lost its bling!" Ever wonder where it got its bling to begin with? Russian czar Alexander II wanted to serve his guests a champagne that was unavailable anywhere else. He went to Louis Roederer, who developed the first "Prestige Cuvée," a blend from its best vineyards, and put it in lead crystal bottles. Thus was Cristal born.

Champagne is just as much a status symbol as it is a libation. James Bond drinks Taittinger, not shaken *or* stirred. Winston Churchill enjoyed a bottle of Pol Roger every day. Napoleon and George Washington drank Moët, although never in the same room. Cristal has been loved by both rappers and royalty alike.

Sadly, since I've never won a NASCAR event or been the world champion of anything, I have never had the privilege of spraying champagne on anyone's head. And since I do not have a boat, I have not had the pleasure of breaking a magnum across a brand-new hull. Thus, before I went to France, my only experiences with champagne consisted of toasting with it at weddings and chugging it at New Year's Eve parties. My knowledge of champagne was limited before I visited Champagne. And much of what I knew was wrong. But now I know the facts. And in just a few pages, so will you.

The Church of Bubbles

In 1668, a young monk came to the Abbaye de Hautvillers monastery to revive their decrepit vineyards. For many years, monks had been the primary producers of booze, making alcoholic beverages as a disease-free alternative to stagnant and dirty water supplies. Young Pierre, whose last name was Pérignon (sound familiar?), experimented with adding carbonation to wine, creating a bubbly cousin to the long-favored still wines that were originally produced in the region of Champagne. When he had his first sip of the bubbly he reportedly cried out, "Je bois les étoiles!" ("I am drinking the stars!")

Dom Pierre Pérignon's experiments in sparkling wine created some new bottling challenges. The pressure of the carbonation that built up inside the bottles would often cause them to burst. And if the glass didn't explode, the bottles were still prone to popping their lids, spontaneously firing corks in a chain reaction throughout the cellar. It is said that these cork-flying events would often destroy up to 90 percent of Dom Pérignon's inventory. So the monk got smart and devised some solutions. He created a bottle with a more sturdy shape and a concaved "punt" (the technical term for the bottom of the bottle) to withstand the extreme pressure, thus becoming the inventor of the modern-day champagne bottle. He also came up with a wire "cage" or "muzzle" to keep the cork secure.

Pérignon's inventions paved the way for today's champagne, but despite these and other contributions, the Dom remained a little-known figure in the modern world of champagne until Moët & Chandon acquired the rights to his name and plastered "Dom Pérignon" on one of their blends back in 1936, more

The cork inserted into champagne bottles is cylindrical. The pressure from the bottle is what forms it into the shape of a mushroom.

than two hundred years after his death. The rest is history, and to this day *Dom Pérignon* is synonymous with "fine champagne."

It is worth mentioning that while the Dom certainly set the bubble in motion, if an individual is to be credited as the official "inventor" of sparkling wine, the distinction should go to a "chap" rather than a "garçon." The first person to intentionally create sparkling wine, back in 1662, was Christopher Merret, an Englishman. There are even mentions of sparkling wine prior to 1662, but they were more accidental concoctions than intentional creations.

Although legend says that Dom Pérignon was blind, many historians disagree. Why the discrepancy? Apparently, once he perfected the blend of grapes used to make his champagne, he often sampled from previous batches to maintain a uniform taste. But he made sure that he didn't know what batch he was drinking from, so he wouldn't skew his assessment. Word soon spread of his "blind" taste tests, and some people took it literally.

Mumm's the Word

The capital of Champagne, France, is the city of Reims, where the Mumm champagne house welcomed me with open arms.

It's worth noting that because Mumm was founded by a German family (Germans are passionate about auto racing), it's the brand of champagne that NASCAR racers are famous for spraying in victory. And because Mumm is located in Reims, thirty minutes north of Epernay, there are some champagne snobs who don't consider Mumm as authentically "French" as some other champagnes. But that doesn't seem to bother them, or their customers: Mumm is the third-biggest supplier of champagne throughout the world.

The scarlet slash on Mumm champagne bottles represents France's highest badge of honor, the ribbon of the Légion d'Honneur.

While Reims is the official capital of the region, the self-proclaimed "capital of Champagne," for both the region and the sparkling wine, is Epernay. At the center of the pomp and spectacle of the town is Rue de Champagne, "Champagne Road." This regal road is lined with opulent buildings bearing the gilded monikers of Champagne's most treasured labels. Moët & Chandon, Perrier-Jouët, Charbaut, De Venoge, and Pol Roger are among the many top-notch champagne houses.

But the choice to put it there was strictly a marketing decision. It doesn't signify any award or medal. Mumm just thought it made their labels look classy. (It's like combing my hair and putting me in a tuxedo—makes me look fancy.) However, I am pleased to report that they abide by all of the champagne-making standards set forth by the CIVC, the Comité Interprofessionnel du Vin de Champagne (whom I lovingly call the "champagne police"), and have been doing so since 1827.

Mumm's metropolitan estate is super-impressive. The buildings are large and old and echo magnificently. But the real showstopper isn't *in* the buildings, it's beneath them. Like most of the champagne houses throughout Champagne, Mumm is situated directly above the entrance to a labyrinth of underground caves where their champagne bottles are kept for maturation. These "chalk caves" are man-made tunnels through an ancient seabed, which time has turned into chalk.

While walking the chalk caves at Mumm's, I was invited by my guide to carve my name in the soft chalk. I happily obliged as I pulled out my rental car key and etched ZANE into the wall. She assured me that I was not defacing the property. Surprisingly, that did not make it less fun.

There are over a hundred miles of tunnels carved into the chalk under Reims and Epernay. Back in the days before temperature-controlled chambers, chalk caves were not only the *best* way to maintain a constant cool temperature throughout the year, they were the *only* way. The cool air allows the champagne to age more predictably, important when your champagne might have wound up on the king's dining table.

HOW TO OPEN A BOTTLE OF CHAMPAGNE

The waiter at Café du Palais opened a bottle of Moët & Chandon without the cork making any sound...at all. Astounding! But that's the civilized way to do it.

TYPICAL:

The celebratory explosion-style of popping the cork can waste about a glass of champagne, and the cork, which can travel at 40 mph, can be dangerous.

IMPRESSIVE:

Open the bottle in silence. To do so, avoid agitating the bottle. Keep your thumb on the cork and untwist the wire cage. When removing the cage from the bottle, you'll have to remove your thumb for a second. Once the cage is safely removed, hold the cork firmly in your hand and slowly wag it back and forth. You'll hear a slight hiss as the pressure is released.

IMPRESSIVE BUT DANGEROUS:

Open the bottle with a saber! As I did with Conan O'Brien on *The Tonight Show*, you simply lop off the top of the bottle with your blade. The blade can be dull, but having a heavier blade is advantageous. Holding the bottle at 45 degrees, find the seam and have it facing up; place the blade on the bottle and slide up the neck in one motion. You're not removing the cork, but rather the entire top of the bottle. The trick, and most important step, is to pre-chill the neck of the bottle in ice, making the glass more brittle. Without this step, you're asking for trouble.

HOW TO OPEN CHAMPAGNE WITH A SABER

1. Always make sure the neck of your bottle is thoroughly chilled.

2. Undress the bottle. During this step, it's best to talk dirty to it as well.

3. Remove the cage and place your thumb on the cork. I've had corks explode on me before.

4. Line the saber along the seam of the bottle and slide the blade up the bottle.

5. When done, you've removed not only the cork, but the end of the bottle as well.

MOST IMPRESSIVE, MOST DANGEROUS:

When the neck is chilled, it's extremely volatile. In this state, and with a bit of practice, you could even open the bottle with a pencil. But the most impressive way is with the bottom of a champagne flute. Tap the ridge at the top of the bottle (where you would strike with a saber) with the bottom of the champagne glass a few times.

> Then give it a nice, strong tap. It's dangerous, so don't try it! That being said, I did it and it's extremely cool. It made me cooler than I really am, even if only for a moment.

Size Matters! (And So Does Location)

I learned two important things about champagne in Champagne. The trick to expensive champagne is the size of the bubbles. Expensive champagnes typically contain smaller bubbles than champagnes of lesser quality. Remember, there's no such thing as bad champagne, just better champage! The larger bubbles, called "tigers' eyes," are often found in champagnes that have aged for the minimum fifteen months. A general rule is "The smaller the bubbles, the smoother the champagne."

The second thing I learned is that if it wasn't made in Champagne, it doesn't matter how good the bubbles taste ... it's not champagne. It's sparkling wine.

According to the CIVC, in order to call it champagne, growers must also adhere to strict guidelines dictating such things as planting, pruning, harvesting, pressing, and how it is handled and aged. There are other methods for making sparkling wine, but the CIVC fights to uphold champagne's distinction. They've even fought among themselves.

The current champagne-making region, as defined by the CIVC, includes the departments (counties) of Marne, Aisne, and Aube. In December 1908, a decree was passed stating that sparkling wine could be called champagne only if it hailed from Marne and Aisne. This didn't sit well with the farmers in Aube, since they had been making champagne prior to that and depended on its distinction for their livelihood. Then, in 1911, further penalties were issued for growers in Marne and Aisne who brought in grapes from Aube for their champagne. This pushed the farmers from Aube over the edge and five thousand of them stormed into the "official" Champagne region and destroyed everything in their path, including six million bottles of champagne. Order was eventually restored, and Aube was once again allowed to continue providing grapes for champagne.

In the United States, the rules aren't as strict. You can thank the U.S. Senate for the more lax guidelines: After President Woodrow Wilson signed the Treaty of Versailles, the Senate never ratified it. Since the treaty is unenforceable, the word *champagne* may be used on bottles of sparkling wine made in the United States, but must be done so with clever wording. So if you buy a bottle of Korbel because it says "champagne" on the label, look again: It's made in California.

CHAMPAGNE VS. SPARKLING WINE

Italy	Moscato, prosecco, and franciacorta are effervescent alternatives to champagne.
Spain	To appease the CIVC, Spain changed the name of its sparklers from champán to cava, meaning cave, in 1970.
United States	Some American companies dress up their sparkling wine as if it's the real deal. Next time you go to the store to pick up some bubbly, look carefully for phrases like "méthod champenoise" or

	"California champagne"—and if you're looking for authentic champagne, avoid them, but some can be quite good.
Germany	Sekt is a respected sparkling wine made with high German standards.
New Zealand	The Kiwis make a variety of sparkling wines most commonly labeled "méthode traditionelle."
Australia	As wine down under grows in popularity, so does their production of sparkling wine.
France	Outside Champagne, it's just sparkling French wine. It can be made the same way, with the same grapes, but if it ain't done in Champagne, it ain't called champagne.

The Champagne Sippy-Cup

The traditions passed on through the generations are what make champagne so exceptional, and that's no more evident than by visiting Godmé Père et Fils, a small, family-owned champagne operation in Verzy. Beneath their champagne factory, which also serves as the family's house, is their cave, where you can still see ridges left behind by the handheld carving knives their ancestors used to manually excavate the chalk one scoop at a time. The caves are so old that the family doesn't even know how long they've owned them. Visiting Godmé leaves you feeling like you've scratched beneath the formal hype and finally dug into the blood and toil of champagne. Even more significantly, you'll also discover that real men really *do* drink champagne. And how.

In fact, the Godmé men drank so much champagne that, generations ago, the women of the family were not pleased that the men would always return from the bottling room half-cocked from all the "quality and control testing." To stop the men from imbibing, they took all of the champagne flutes out of the bottling room. As married men must do, they succumbed to their wives' requests and allowed their flutes to be confiscated. But, as I was shown, the cavity at the base of an empty champagne bottle makes the perfect emergency goblet. As soon as the ladies had left them to their work, the men simply flipped the bottles over and it was back to business as usual.

In a Glass

You may have heard that the champagne flute was originally shaped like the breast of Marie Antoinette. If so, you've been misled. First of all, a breast shaped like a contemporary champagne flute could probably take an eye out. Yikes! Second of all, the legend actually refers to the "champagne coupe," a stemmed glass with the shape of a shallow bowl that is also used for drinking champagne. However, the coupe was designed in England in 1663, well before little Marie was ever born.

Nowadays we use the crystal flute instead of the curvy coupe because it's better for the bubbles. And after all, that's the point of champagne. Without the bubbles, it would just be wine. The preferred material for flutes is crystal because it has more natural imperfections than glass. The tiny imperfections catch the CO_2 as it rises and

How many bubbles does a bottle of champagne have? Scientist Bill Lembeck crunched the numbers and concluded that the quantity of bubbles in the average bottle of champagne is around 49 million. Then computer geek Bruno Dutertre came along, funded in part by Moët, and determined using a computer-based camera system that the average bottle of champagne contains as many as 250 million bubbles. Wow, you showed him, Bruno ... Showed him what a colossal nerd you are.

HOW TO MAKE A MIMOSA

The mimosa, staple of country club brunches and first-class cabins, was invented at the Ritz Carlton in Paris in 1925.

Pour two parts orange juice into a champagne flute.

Top off with one part champagne and a dash of old-money snobbery.

turns the accumulated gas into bubbles. In contrast, a perfectly smooth glass (which is basically impossible) would have no bubbles at all. The long stem of a flute is also important because it prevents your hand from warming the chilled champagne.

Let's Get Technical

Now that you get what champagne is about, here's some information that you may think will impress your friends but will actually bore the shit out of them.

Bottles come in a wide array of sizes. Although most are the standard 750 ml bottles, the larger bottles are as impressive as their names. Next time you're at a party, tell them that you were going to bring a Nebuchadnezzar but didn't have anyone to help you carry it. They won't know what you're talking about, but you'll know it's hilarious.

Bottle	Capacity	Equivalent
Standard bottle	.75 liters	1 bottle
Magnum	1.5 liters	2 bottles
Jeroboam	3 liters	4 bottles
Rehoboam	4.5 liters	6 bottles
Methuselah	6 liters	8 bottles
Salmanazar	9 liters	12 bottles
Balthazar	12 liters	16 bottles
Nebuchadnezzar	15 liters	20 bottles
Solomon	20 liters	28 bottles
Primat	27 liters	36 bottles

Process

Champagne is made by a double fermentation process. The first fermentation takes place in a vat, as with any other wine. But the resulting product is highly acidic and wouldn't taste too good. The second fermentation occurs in the bottle, when yeast and sugar are introduced to the still wine. The by-product of yeast eating sugar is

DOM Your Name Here

**HOW TO CREATE
YOUR OWN "CHAMPAGNE"**
(just please don't call it that in public)

Start with a bottle of chardonnay.

Add the juice from one lemon to increase the acidity.

Add one teaspoon of sugar and ¼ teaspoon of brewer's yeast to kick-start the carbonation process.

The final step is corking the bottle to push the CO_2 back into the wine.

The Wrong Way: Do *not* use the original bottle. If you use the bottle the wine came in, within a short time, your cork will most likely be pushed out of the bottle (or your bottle will be reduced to a pile of wet, broken glass). You will be creating a time bomb and your significant other/roommates/pets will not be pleased.

The Right Way: Instead, pour your mixture into an empty champagne bottle, and cap it with a cork and cage. Voilà!

alcohol and CO_2. The bottle is then sealed and left to age upside down in a chalk cave, where it is riddled (gently shaken and rotated) regularly, for a minimum of one and a half years. This riddling helps the yeast to settle into the neck of the bottle, forming the "lees."

Once the bottle is fully matured, the inverted neck is then frozen, and in one quick movement, the bottle is opened and the frozen lees pop out like a cork. The sediment-free bottle is then quickly corked to prevent further loss of carbonation, until opened for consumption.

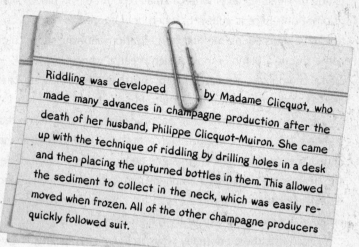

Riddling was developed by Madame Clicquot, who made many advances in champagne production after the death of her husband, Philippe Clicquot-Muiron. She came up with the technique of riddling by drilling holes in a desk and then placing the upturned bottles in them. This allowed the sediment to collect in the neck, which was easily removed when frozen. All of the other champagne producers quickly followed suit.

How Do You Doux

As per the CIVC, in order for a wine to be called champagne, it must be made from a combination of three grapes: pinot noir, pinot meunier, and chardonnay (although a few others are allowed in certain quanities). The grapes must come from predetermined areas in Marne, Aisne, and Aube. Only the chardonnay is a green grape. The other two are red or, more appropriately, "purple" grapes.

Back when Dom Pérignon was perfecting his champagne method, he found that a wine press that squeezed the grapes no harder than the pressure created when pinching a grape between your thumb and index finger produced the best results. In this manner, which is still followed today, the juice is extracted without picking up much of the color from the grape skins.

Champagne is either a *blanc de blanc,* or a *rosé,* or a *blanc de noir*. Blanc de blanc means "white from white." Blanc de blanc champagne is made exclusively from chardonnay. A rosé is a pink champagne that gets its color when a small amount of red pinot meunier or pinot noir juice is added, or when brief contact is made with the red grape skins during the first fermentation, allowing some color to come through. Blanc de noir, which means "white from black," is a white champagne squeezed from the grape so delicately that it doesn't take on any color from the skin.

The sweetness of the champagne, called the doux, is created by adding sugar during the second fermentation. The more sugar that is added, the less "dry" the champagne becomes. The doux and "demisec" (moderately sweet) champagnes are most often consumed as dessert wines. And the more expensive champagnes (the ones you order when you want to look like a high-roller) are "bruts."

Of course, there are many ways to judge champagne. The word *cru* is used to refer to the quality of grapes used to make any given champagne, which is typically a blend of various grapes taken from different vineyards. The vineyard's slope,

TERROIR: Environmental factors within a given area that influence the development of grape varietals.

position to the sun, and soil makeup are among the categories of distinction, factoring into what is called the *terroir*. *Terroir* is a French term for a "sense of place." Wine aficionados use it to describe soil, climate, and topography of a region—anything that can affect the way the grapes will taste. And the attention to terroir can be intense: An individual row of grapevines can be said to have its own terroir.

If everything is tip-top, the vineyard receives a mark of 100 percent and is given the distinction as a "Grand Cru" vineyard. A score of a still-respectable 90 to 99 percent is considered "Premier Cru." And

CHAMPAGNE SWEETNESS

Doux	Sweet. Usually used as a dessert wine. 5 percent or more residual sugar.
Demi-sec	Partially dry, but still noticeably sweet. 3.5–5 percent residual sugar.
Sec	Dry, with a hint of sweetness. 1.7–3.5 percent residual sugar.
Extra sec	Extra dry. Well balanced. 1.2–2.0 percent residual sugar.
Brut	Nearly completely dry. 1.5 percent residual sugar. The premier champagnes are bruts: Perrier-Jouët, Dom Pérignon, Cristal, Taittinger, Krug, etc.
Extra brut, brut zero, ultra brut, brut sauvage, brut nature, brut intégral	Completely dry. No sugar added; 0.6 percent residual sugar. Many of the fine champagne makers also make an extra brut.

"Cru Normal" is anything less than 89 percent. Expensive champagne is most often from grapes of Grand Cru vineyards.

Since champagne is often made with a blend of several years' grapes, it is not as important to keep track of a certain year as you would with most wines. Even a "vintage" only has to be 80 percent from that year. This is done so that champagne from other years can balance it out, giving the champagne a more consistent taste year to year.

Le Hangover

In Champagne, they say that if you're drinking champagne (as opposed to sparkling wine), you won't get a hangover. At least a dozen people made this claim to me while I was visiting Reims. Now, if there's one thing I know, it's that an alcoholic beverage taken in excess, no matter how steeped in tradition it may be, or how astronomical the price, will inexorably cause a hangover.

In Reims, the perfect place to put this to the test is Café du Palais, a champagne bar that looks like the French equivalent to an upscale Irish pub with a lot of art. On my visit, the owner, Jean-François, was kind enough to indulge my barrage of questions. But when I got around to the seemingly outlandish claim that people had been making about champagne not causing hangovers, he declared it to be true.

> **Me:** So I can drink several glasses of champagne, and get absolutely no hangover?
>
> **Jean-François:** Of course, you'd get no hangover from ten glasses.

And there it was. He threw down the gauntlet—or the champagne flute—or whatever. Here was the perfect opportunity to set the record straight. Jean-François agreed to join me on my new mission and we promptly ordered up a few bottles of the good stuff. (No strawberries, though: Jean-François prefers to accompany a glass with one of the small toasted cheese sandwiches that his mother makes and serves at his bar.)

We got one of the house bottles, "Champagne a Café du Palais," a bottle of Moët (at which point I learned it was pronounced "mo-ET") and a bottle of Cristal ('cause that's how I roll). Each arrived in its own icy bucket. In the end, I put away eleven glasses of champagne, which is five glasses more than a bottle, but only two glasses short of a magnum. I was pretty well lit.

So was Jean-Francois correct? No. Can champagne give you a hangover? *Hell yes*. The next morning, I was indeed hungover. I didn't feel like dancing, drinking, or being vertical for an extended period of time. I wanted to eat and then crawl back in bed.

Hangover Soup

It was suggested that for a hangover remedy I try French onion soup, which of course in France is just called onion soup. The soup had no medicinal qualities, no caffeine, and it didn't have any hair of the dog. It merely warmed my belly, filled my stomach, and made for a nice brunch, but as for relieving any of my symptoms, it had very little effect.

Remedy rating: *One out of Three Sheets. Skip the soup, order room service.*

Chapter 3

Scotland

Latitude: 57°00' N

Longitude: 4°00' W

What they call it: Scotland (English and Scots), Alba (Gaelic)

What they speak: English, Scottish Gaelic, Scots

How to say cheers: *Sláinte mhath!* (Gaelic for "good health"; if someone says that to you, the correct response is *Sláinte mhor*, which means "great health") and "Cheers!"

Hangover remedy: Haggis!

SCOTLAND

Highlands

Edinburgh

Lowlands

Scotland (SCOT-lund) 1. The second-largest country in Great Britain. 2. The whisky capital of the known universe. 3. One of the few parts of the world where manly men strut around in skirts.

Some people go to Scotland for the history, warm winters (kidding), and a certain mythical beast. But the main draw, for me at least, is the plethora of superb whiskies available across the highlands, lowlands, and all the lands in between.

As with beer and loads of other alcoholic ambrosias, cereal isn't just an accompaniment to Saturday morning cartoons. In Scotland, the same thing that you had in your bowl this morning is what you'll be quaffing at happy hour. Whisky, like Irish whiskey, is an alcoholic beverage that is made from the distillation of grains (cereal)—barley, malted barley, rye, malted rye, wheat, and corn (maize)—and then aged in oak barrels for at least a year, but most often longer.

Distillation

While the creation of alcohol through fermentation has been around for several millennia, distillation is only centuries old. Distillation is the process by which alcohol is removed from a fermented liquid. In the case of whisky, it starts with what is basically beer, but without the hops. The still heats the "beer" to a boil, causing the alcohol to evaporate. Alcohol evaporates at a lower temperature (173 degrees Fahrenheit) than water. This gaseous form of alcohol rises to the top of the still and condenses, returning it to a liquid. The liquid then drips down a separate tube to where it is collected, and in the case of whiskey the process is repeated one or two more times until the alcohol reaches a certain level of purity. With whiskey, the clear liquid is then diluted to around 40 percent alcohol with spring water and aged in charred oak barrels. In this process it picks up the colors and flavors of the burnt oak and the barrel's original tenants (as they are often used wine or brandy barrels).

Hold the E

While the Scottish maintain Scotch whisky is better than Irish whiskey, the Irish understandably disagree. But both the Irish and the

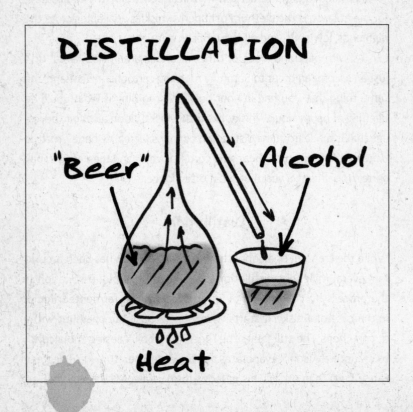

DISTILLATION

"Beer" Alcohol

Heat

Scottish agree that it was Ireland that invented the stuff. One legend, although strongly disputed by historians, says that St. Patrick is re-

Date

Until early in the eighteenth century, the Kingdom of Scotland was an independent sovereign state. The year 2007 marked three hundred years of being part of the Kingdom of Great Britain. However, they've done a very impressive job of maintaining their unique culture. From politics to drinking, the Scots have an identity distinct from England, Wales, and Northern Ireland; it is characterized by their own legal system, skirts for men, and their own special way of spelling whisky. Some people are still not pleased about the 1707 join-up. Among them is actor Sean Connery, one of today's best-known Scots, who has "Scotland Forever" tattooed on his arm and believes that Scotland will receive its independence from the United Kingdom in his lifetime. He's got a better chance at playing a geriatric Agent 007.

sponsible for bringing the knowledge of whisky distillation from Ireland to Scotland.

The first written record of Scotch was from a friar, John Cor, in 1495, in the "Exchequer Rolls of Scotland." Back in the day, monasteries would distill small quantities of whisky for medicinal purposes. But in the fifteenth century, when many monasteries closed down, the monks, who had acquired a marketable skill, were then forced to distill in order to make a living. Their knowledge of distillation, no longer kept quiet in monasteries, quickly spread around the country, and the quality of Scotch production improved.

The Scotch industry got a leg up in 1880, when France fell under attack by North America. It wasn't an army of men, but the accidental introduction of an aphidlike insect that may have been introduced from a North American vine. This pest, called the phylloxera, attacked helpless grapevines in France, severely affecting the production of brandy (including cognac), and leaving Scotch to fill the temporary void. Scotch did such a good job of replacing the demand that the brandy industry has never regained its reigning position.

What Makes It Scotch?

Just as champagne and tequila have geographical and technical requirements to be called such, Scotch has guidelines that must be followed if the final product is to be called "Scotch whisky."

The first and most obvious requirement is that the distillery in which it's produced must be in Scotland. Additionally, it must be made solely from water, malted barley, and yeast, with the acceptable addition of whole grains. Scotch much be matured in oak casks for no less than three years. It must be distilled to no more than 94.8 percent alcohol so it retains some of the residual flavors, and bottled at no less than 40 percent alcohol (80 proof) after it has been "cut" by mixing it with water.

THE 19TH HOLE

Golfers have debated for centuries as to why there are eighteen holes on a golf course. At St. Andrews, home to the prestigious British Open, legend has it that there's no coincidence that it takes eighteen swigs to polish off a bottle of whisky. Golfers, it was once said, should be able to get in one swig per hole, and be done when the bottle is empty. Nice story, but anyone who's ever played a round of golf, or tried to finish a bottle of alcohol, knows that the two are tough enough on their own without combining them. The _19th hole_, is what golfers call the club bar.

Scotch is divided into four categories: single malt, single grain, vatted malt, and blended.

Single malt whisky is made solely with malted barley in pot stills and must be made at one single distillery. It must be aged in oak barrels for a minimum of three years.

Single grain whisky is also distilled at a single distillery from malted barley. But in contrast to single malt whisky, it may contain other whole grains. The majority of single grain whisky is produced to be part of a **blended whisky.** A pure single grain whisky is not that common; you would need some resourcefulness to find one.

Vatted or **pure malt whiskies** are another lesser-known Scotch. They are a blend of single malt whiskies from two or more distilleries and from different years. No distillery is noted on the bottle, and the word *single* is absent because the makers combined several singles, which voids that description. When different years are combined, the youngest year is printed on the bottle.

Blended whisky is simply a blend of single malt whiskies from two or more distilleries. Over 90 percent of the whisky made in Scotland is blended. Being able to combine different single malt and single grain whiskies from different distilleries and different batches enables the master distillers to produce a more uniform product consistent from year to year. Dewar's and Johnny Walker are examples of blended whiskies.

Blended grain whisky is a fusion of single grain whiskies from two or more distilleries.

Blended Scotch whisky is a merging of single malt whiskies and single grain whiskies from more than one distillery.

Scotch whiskies also vary depending on their geographical location and the kind of water used to make them.

Looking at a Glenfiddich bottle from the bottom, you will see that it is not round, but rather triangular. Legend has it that the original owner loved the whisky so much that he brought a bottle of it to bed with him every night. But when he woke up the next morning, the bottle would always have rolled on the floor for him to trip on. So he reportedly asked the bottle manufacturer to make a bottle that wouldn't roll out of bed...

Speyside: The distilleries in Speyside, where Glenfiddich is located, use fresh mountain runoff water in their product, which gives it a "velvety smooth" taste.

Lowlands: The lowlands, located near Edinburgh, use rainwater from local rivers in their product. You've tasted a lowlands malt if you've ever had Johnny Walker Red or Black Label.

Islay: In the west of Scotland is Islay, where the ground is very "peaty." Fallen trees, branches, and leaves slowly decompose in the soil, forming peat. The water falls as rain and seeps through the peat, giving Islay Scotch an earthy taste. You can try a single malt of Islay from McClelland.

The **island of Skye**, to the northwest, uses mountain springwater to make classics like Talisker.

The **Orkney Islands** use water pulled from artesian wells that can be three thousand feet deep; the results are bottled in Scotches such as Highland Park.

HOW TO MAKE A RUSTY NAIL

Drambuie is an 80-proof liqueur made from Scotch whisky, honey, and a "secret blend of herbs and spices." It can be served straight up, over ice, or in its best-known form, a Rusty Nail.

Fill a glass with ice.

Add 1.5 ounces of Scotch.

Add a half ounce of Drambuie.

Add a lemon twist.

Note: Consuming a Rusty Nail does not require a tetanus shot.

With Age Comes...a High Price Tag

One could spend an exorbitant amount of time and money traveling around Scotland, visiting its whisky distilleries. I chose to visit Glenfiddich, a Speyside single malt Scotch whisky distillery that has been around since 1876 and is home to the world's bestselling single malt.

At Glenfiddich, they sell Scotch at a wide range of ages, including their pièce de résistance, a fifty-year-old granddaddy that I couldn't wait to get my hands on. In recent years, I'd tried a bevy of expensive drinks. Generally they're expensive because they (or their ingredients) are rare or old or purely because of a marketing ploy to promote something as being expensive. With the Glenfiddich fifty-year-old single malt Scotch whisky, all of those apply. In their gift shop, they sell a bottle of the 50, in its oak case, with brass plaque and satin lining, for around ten thousand dollars. That's a hefty chunk of change. Is it a product that people are expected to buy or is it for bragging rights so the distillery can say that they carry a ten-thousand-dollar bottle of booze? Or is it for

In the movie *Braveheart*, Mel Gibson played William Wallace, leader of a growing army of rebellious Scotsmen fighting for independence in the late thirteenth century. While his movement eventually succeeds, Wallace himself is tortured and killed (if that ruined the movie for you, then you should consider seeing Academy Award–winning films within a decade of their release). Much of the movie was shot in Scotland, but the major battle scenes were shot in Ireland, using members of the Irish Army Reserve as extras (up to 1,600 in some scenes). They all received permission from the army to grow beards so that they looked like soldiers from "back in the day."

DRAM: The word *dram* comes from *drachm,* which used to be a Greek and Roman reference to either a coin or a weight. Today the term is used less formally to mean a small amount of liquid—usually Scotch.

special guests to try, and then feel appreciative for the privilege of having a five-hundred-dollar dram?

I tried their fifteen-year-old whisky, their 25, and their 50. And my relatively humble and inexperienced opinion is that the fifty-year-old Scotch did taste the best. But it's kinda like buying a TV at Best Buy. Sure, the ten-thousand-dollar, 60-inch Sony looked better than the three-thousand-dollar, 50-inch brand I'd never heard of. Stay clear of the Yokono sets. But without having another TV to compare it with when I get it home, would I really notice the difference? Glenfiddich's 25 was definitely superior to the 15. But the discrepancy was far less between the 25 and the 50. So while the 50 was better (in terms of what makes an older Scotch "better"), it did not come close to reflecting the divergence in the price. The 25 is easily found at most liquor stores and can be yours for about three hundred dollars. The 50 comes in an oak box, with a brass plaque, and is produced in very limited quantities. Sure, the 50 was smoother. Smoother than I was when I balked at the price.

How to Order Whisky Like a Professional

The Quaich Bar, located at the Craigellachi Hotel, just down the road from Glenfiddich, has one of the best selections of Scotches in the world. In fact, it's difficult to say whether there's any bar in the world that has a better selection. With 659 different Scotches on hand, it's highly unlikely. Besides, this place rents out rooms, so it's the perfect place for both sampling and oversampling

A quaich, or "loving cup," is a two-handled silver bowl that is traditionally used for drinking Scotch. It can be passed around and shared, or enjoyed on your own. The silver color makes it easy to examine the caramel color of the whisky; however, original quaichs were carved from wood. It's thought that the design was formed in the shape of large scallop shells, which were reportedly used for consuming drams in the early days of whisky distillation. When you're ordering up your whisky
(or pouring it yourself,
once you get the

The Keepers of the Quaich is a club established by Scotch distillers to advance their industry and contribute to charities. They currently boast more than 1,800 members. Membership, which is by invitation only, is reserved for those who have made a significant contribution to the whisky industry.

hang of it), it's good to know that a dram is a single pour of Scotch. It's an unmeasured unit but is usually around an ounce and a half (depending on who's doing the pouring). You can also ask for a unit of Scotch called a finger. You fill a glass to the width of your finger when gripping the glass, and up to four fingers (which is a very generous pour). Anything over two fingers would be considered generous. Depending on the width of the glass and your sausage fingers, that would be between two and three ounces.

Breaking The Law

Edinburgh, in case you weren't paying attention in the eighth grade, is the capital of Scotland. The city of Glasgow is slightly larger, but in Scotland, at least, size isn't everything: Edinburgh gets the seat of government and most of the seats of tourists, too.

If you fancy Scotch, Scotland, or a good time, the historic Royal Mile in Edinburgh is a necessary destina-tion. And for a really great experience in whisky educa-tion, you might head (very log-ically) to a bar named Whiski.

On my re-cent visit, I sam-pled something that's illegal in the United States. It's a Glenfiddich Grand Reserve 21 that's been aged in oak barrels and (here's the danger-ous part) has been "finished" in Cuban rum barrels. It is ille-gal to bring anything Cuban-made into the United States. Obviously, by drinking this stuff I was supporting the communist movement and thereby carelessly endangering the free world. But I was thirsty... The rum taste is slight, but it is noticeable. I rather enjoyed it—if that's okay with you. Please don't brand me a pinko commie... For the record, the dram I had was free. So technically I'm still a good American.

I was also told by a customer that to truly enjoy a whisky, it should be mixed not with ice cubes, but an equal part of warm water. The idea is that by reducing the alcohol proof, you better taste the nuances of the Scotch. And by golly, it worked! Back in the United States, I usually drink Scotch on the rocks. But by chilling the Scotch, I'm effectively taking some of the flavor away. I was also told to take some air in with my sip (basically slurping the Scotch) to allow more oxygen into my mouth and thus better taste it. That, too, works. But I don't do that back in the States, either. What's wrong with me?!

Got Guts?

For the traditionalist: Bite the bullet, or in this case, a bloated sheep's stomach. The national "dish" of Scotland, haggis, is a sheep's intestine filled with the sheep's minced organs mixed with spices and oatmeal and then boiled. Other than the fact that it's traditionally served with "neeps and tatties" (turnips and potatoes), it's basically what it sounds like. And it reportedly tastes like that, too. At Whiski, they serve up a modern version of haggis. It's finely minced and spiced to the point where the organs and taste are indistinguishable. I'd say it tasted good, but I couldn't stop thinking about the ingredients...

Remedy rating: *One out of Three Sheets. Something that makes you sick to your stomach before you even eat it won't do much to reduce your nausea.*

Chapter 4

Belgium

Latitude: 50°50' N

Longitude: 4°00' E

Capital: Brussels

What they call it: België (Dutch), Belgique (French), Belgien (German)

What they speak: Dutch, French, and German

How to say cheers: *Op uw gezondheid!* (Dutch) or *Santé!* (French) or *Prost!* (German)

Hangover remedy: Chocolate or mussels (but not at the same time…ew…)

Belgium (BEL-jum) 1. Home of Brussels, capital of the European Union. 2. A country where, when the water was unsafe, they drank beer. 3. A place where someone thought infusing gin with Brussels sprouts was a good idea... It was not.

In Belgium, they take their beer seriously. So seriously that they're happy to waste it just to make you happier. Bartenders will often overfill your glass so the foams runneth over. They then scrape the remaining foam off with a dull knife. This is said to help the beer release its bouquet, which is said to enhance your drinking experience. This fact alone is enough reason for any beer drinker to make the pilgrimage to Belgium.

A Mecca for Beer Lovers

If you do go to Belgium, don't drink the water...drink the beer. That's advice that you would have gotten half a century ago—and I'm still standing behind it today. Until about fifty years ago, the river that ran through Brussels, the capital city, was highly polluted, which affected the stagnant water tables in the surrounding areas. So one of the best ways to get a clean drink was to obtain an inexpensively purified libation: beer. The Belgians brewed beer as a safe alternative to the bad H_2O, proving that good things really can flow from bad waters.

Because of its sudsy past, Belgium is the place to go if you worship beer. Today the country produces more than one thousand different beers, many in the traditional styles, such as Lambic and Trappist beers, making it the perfect place for a religious drinking experience.

Beer 101: The Ingredients

Most beer is made with four simple ingredients: water, barley, yeast, and hops. Other ingredients are often used, but these are the necessary ones.

Water is the main ingredient in beer. Its source can affect the taste of the beer. For this reason, the water used by major companies with breweries in different countries, such as Guinness, is regulated so the beer will have a consistent taste.

Malted barley is the second most popular ingredient in beer. Other grains can be added, such as rice. But the basic starch in beer is malted barley. Barley that is "malted" is soaked in water to let it germinate. Then, just when it's about to sprout a leaf, it's cooked and mercilessly killed.

Hops is a flower (albeit not a pretty one) that grows on vines and was originally used as a preservative but is now considered a significant flavor element. Its bitterness is said to balance the sweetness of the malted barley. The acidity and natural oils of hops make it a good preservative and give beer its characteristic foamy head.

Brewer's yeast is a living microorganism that is the key component in the fermentation process. Very simply put, the yeast eats the sugars and then poops out alcohol and carbon dioxide. With pasteurized beer, the yeast is usually killed off, halting the fermentation process.

Beer 201: Combining the Ingredients

Beer is delicious. If you've never tried it, I highly recommend picking some up. If you are resourceful enough, you should be able to find it locally in your community. Ask around. After tea and water (another beverage you just gotta try), beer is the most commonly consumed beverage in the world. It's both the world's first alcoholic beverage and its most widely consumed. The Egyptians are credited with creating beer more than nine thousand years ago, to which I offer them my humble thanks. Between that, domesticated cats (for funny YouTube videos), and the pyramids, I think we can all agree that Egypt has done its part.

The recipe for beer basically boils down to boiled cereal with some hops and yeast thrown in. But before you throw the remaining contents of your boxes of Cheerios and Special K into a pot of water,

I should clarify: Producing a palatable beer is a complicated scientific process that is difficult to lock down and even more difficult to duplicate. The ingredients are simple, but not so the process that turns grains into a delectable and drinkable ambrosia that has been gladdening hearts and lips ever since Cleopatra thought that a snake would make a nice accessory for her gown. For the purposes of this book, however, I'm going to oversimplify it, potentially pissing off beer snobs everywhere—but those are the chances I'm willing to take to bring you, the dear reader, the highbrow lowdown.

Beer is made by "brewing" grains, and thus converting them from their carbohydrate form into natural sugars. In order to convert anything into alcohol, it must first be converted into sugar. Wine fermentation is easier, since wine is already high in sugar. But beer requires the additional step of brewing (cooking) the malted barley with water to convert it into sugar. This process is called "mashing" and the end product is wort, a sweet liquid.

In Belgium, I learned the German sign for "good burp." When someone burps, the last person who puts their thumb to their head with their pinky in the air has to drink. In St. Martin, they play the same game, but instead of a drink, the loser gets smacked in the forehead. I like the German way better...

The next step, per this simplified explanation, is to separate the grains and add hops. Hops' bitterness balances out the overly sweet wort that was just created. This sweet, hoppy liquid is then cooled because the next ingredient to be added, yeast, is a living organism that will die if overheated. If the yeast dies, so does the beer. Buzz kill! Yeast is so important to beer, and every alcoholic concoction, because the by-product of the yeast eating the sugar is *alcohol* and CO_2. In some brewing processes, the CO_2 is released. But in brewing beer the CO_2 is captured, providing carbonation, those tickly bubbles that make you burp in public. Incidentally, the other by-product, alcohol, is what makes you feel that burping in public is okay.

After a few weeks, or months, depending on the ingredients and specific process, you have beer. Most beer is then pasteurized, which kills the yeast, thereby stopping the production of alcohol. It's then bottled, canned, kegged, casked, jarred, or beer-balled, and it's ready for consumption. Easy, right?

Beer 301: Ales and Lagers

Beers are divided into two main categories: lagers (such as Budweiser, Corona, and Pabst Blue Ribbon) and ales (Guinness, Newcastle, etc). Lager lovers and ale-coholics are sometimes like dog and cat people—suspicious of one another's yearnings and desires, but they go to the same pet stores. So if you're predisposed to one or the other, keep an open mind as you read (or if you've got the topic handy, beer-drink) your way through this chapter.

Lagers are considered bottom-fermented beers because during the fermentation process the yeast sinks to the bottom of the vat. They are fermented at lower temperatures than ales, which makes for more consistency in the final product. They take longer to brew than ales, and are not as sweet. In the United States and United Kingdom, as in many other countries, sales of lagers vastly exceed sales of ales.

Ales are made with top-fermented yeast. This yeast ferments more quickly, making it more full-bodied and sweeter than your common lager. Because of this sweetness, a hearty amount of hops is often added to give the final product a more balanced taste. Ale aficionados tend to turn up their noses at lagers and consider them to be less than flavorful, but that isn't fair to the best of the lagers (although probably more than fair to the blandest of them).

You now know everything that the average person should know about beer. If you learn any more, you'll go from "knowledgeable" to "nerd." Stop reading.

A Good Reason to Join a Monastery

If I were a monk, I'd break my vow of silence in about thirteen seconds, especially if I had a brewery in my backyard, because beer makes me talkative. And celibacy, with free beer? *That's* commitment.

As stated in the Rule of St. Benedict, Trappist monks must "live by the work of their hands." They produce goods that provide them with an income and contribute to their community. Their products are renowned for their quality, and their beer is no exception. While many Trappist monasteries produce food, clothing, and even coffins, six monasteries in Belgium opt to produce beer. Beer connoisseurs and critics agree that Trappist beers are some of the best in the world. The six Trappist abbeys in Belgium that brew beer are Orval, Chimay, Westvleteren, Rochefort, Westmalle, and Achel. Since Trappist beers are nonpasteurized, the yeast continues to produce alcohol while in the bottle. So they're great to begin with *and* are said to improve over time.

In the southern part of the country, a stone's throw from the French border, is one of the most accessible Trappist breweries, Orval, which means "golden valley." On the grounds of the thousand-year-old Orval monastery, they've been making beer since 1931. Like all Trappist beers, Orval's are "top-fermented" ales. Trappist beers vary in alcoholic potency, with titles such as "single," "double," and "triple," referring to the beer's strength. And the pear-shaped Orval bottle is designed so you can pour your beer while leaving behind the sediment. Personally I feel that every ounce should be consumed, and that not consuming the "monk's share" would be a travesty.

If you visit, don't expect to see monks with robes and pronounced bald spots making beer in large wooden barrels. While the monastery next door looks as it did centuries ago, the attached brewery is as modern as any in the business, automated and complete with a lab, publicist, and gift shop. Actually, don't expect to see any monks at all. While they don't take a vow of silence, the monks concern themselves with their religious duties and leave the brewing to the experts. The brewery, run by civilians with degrees and experience in brewing, churns out more than 14 million bottles of beer annually. And despite the fact that they basically live at a brewery, the monks don't drink the commercially available Orval beer produced in their backyard (6.9 percent alcohol). Instead they drink a special brew with a meager alcohol content of around 2 percent.

Orval can be found at most specialty beer stores in the United States, although Chimay is the most easily obtainable. Some other Trappist beers, however, are not so easy to get your hands on. Westvleteren beer, produced by the monks of St. Sixtus of Westvleteren, is said to be one of best beers (if not *the* best) in the world. They make a single, double, and triple, and currently produce a total of a half million cases a year. It's in such demand that the brewery only sells it for individual consumption; each car that visits is allowed to purchase just one case. The monastery frowns on those who would sell it in bars, stores, or online—but that doesn't mean that it doesn't happen. Some consider the triple to be too strong to have more than one of them (okay, maybe two). It's hoppy and a bit heavy, but if that's what you're into, then Westvleteren is your holy grail.

2,004 Bottles of Beer on the Wall

If you want to drink your weight in beer, there's a place in Brussels that you absolutely must visit: the Delirium Café. The sign over the door is adorned with a pink pachyderm, the logo of the Delirium Brewery. But that's just one of the optional brews, because this is a place where you can try every beer you've ever heard of, and a thousand more that you haven't, including their house brew (which is also fairly popular in the United States).

The bar is a friendly place, but a word of warning: Asking the bartender to toss you the beer list might leave you on your ass. Not because of anything that you said or did, but because the menu is the size of a phone book. It contains over two thousand different beers, enough to land the bar in the 2004 Guinness Book of World Records for having the most beers. At any time, since keeping an exact count on the inventory is a chore, they may actually have as many as 2,500 to choose from. This makes the Delirium a great place to sample a wide range of Trappist beers. And once you're done with those, you can make the acquaintance of the often fruitier Lambic family.

On my visit to Delirium, my guide through the beers of Belgium was François, who took me through the paces—as much as my balance could handle . . .

Lambic Beers

After the Trappist beers, Belgium's other significant contribution to the beer world are the Lambics, which must be brewed in the Pajottenland region of Belgium, southwest of Brussels. Lambic beer's unique taste comes from the fact that it is created by "spontaneous fermentation." It's produced in open-top vats, allowing wild yeast to wander into the mixture to begin the fermentation process. It's characterized by its cider flavor, a slightly sour aftertaste, and added fruit flavor.

Lambic beer relies on natural yeasts and bacteria found in the open air of the woody region in which it's made. Production is halted in the summer, because the warm conditions would make the wort too susceptible to harmful bacteria. Similarly to Trappist beers, Lambics use hops as a preservative. But Lambics don't have the same flowery hoppy taste as Trappist brews, because they use less-fragrant dry hops.

Once they have picked up the natural yeasts, Lambics are siphoned into barrels to age for two to three years. After they have matured, Lambics are often sweetened with sugar and fruit.

Fruit Lambics are the most common. They add whole fruit or fruit syrup to the beer during the second fermentation. The most popular fruits are sour cherry (*kriek*),

raspberry (*framboise*), peach (*pêche*), blackcurrant (*cassis*), grape (*druif*), strawberry (*aardbei*), and apple (*pomme*).

My new pal François was gracious enough to break out a bottle of Kriek. The cherry Lambic was so memorably tart that even writing about it is making my my salivary glands kick in. Many Krieks come in champagne-type bottles, which can run upwards of sixty dollars.

Faro Lambics are the least common of the Lambic beers. The modern versions are made with the addition of brown sugar. They are then pasteurized to kill the yeast so it does not ferment the additional sugars.

Gueuze Lambics are made with a mixture of old (two to three years old) and young (one year old) Lambics that undergo a second fermentation in the bottle. These need at least one additional year in the bottle to finish the second fermentation. A gueuze can be kept for ten to twenty years. In contrast, Budweiser removes most of its beer from the shelves if it hasn't sold after 110 days.

Sir! My Beer Is on Fire!

Some Lambics have an alcohol content of only 2.5 percent, half as strong as a typical American beer (Budweiser), and only five times stronger than most nonalcoholic beers (e.g., O'Douls). The Delirium adds a flaming shot of schnapps to its low-alcohol fruity beers, aptly named Flamme de Biére. A note for do-it-yourself-ers: If you tried to

FLASHPOINT: The flashpoint of   alcohol is the point at which it
is flammable. This point, however,   is a formula and not a
consistent number, as it changes based on the temperature of the
liquid. At room temperature (roughly 72 degrees Fahrenheit), a shot
would need to be 120 proof (70 percent alcohol) to ignite. But on a
warm day, or in a warm house (about 84 degrees), you could ignite
"room temperature" alcohol that was 60 proof (30 percent alcohol).
And if it was *really* hot out (about 120 degrees), or you heated the
liquid, you could essentially light a glass of wine on fire. I'm not sure
why you'd want to. But you could. And just in case you *really* want to,
I've included this handy chart, below.

HANDY FLASHPOINT CHART

Proof (Alcohol Percentage x 2)	Temperature of the Liquid (Fahrenheit)
10	144
20	120
40	97
60	84
80	79
100	75
120	72
140	70
160	68
180	63

light your apple schnapps at home, you'd have a bit of trouble. Schnapps in Europe are not like the sugary liqueurs we have in the States. They are much stronger, and have a much lower flash-point.

In Belgium, most beers have their own glass. They have different shapes, different sizes, and different logos. You won't find many pint glasses in Belgian bars, but you will see shelves full of different glasses waiting for their respective beers.

Drink Your Vegetables

One libation that I was served in Brussels should find its flashpoint and stay there until the bottle burns dry. It's called *geniévre aux choux de Bruxelles*, which translates to "gin with Brussels sprouts." The smiling sprout on the label lets you know that a gimmick is needed to peddle this concoction. It has that cabbage and licorice taste that's been missing in gin for centuries. I wonder why. This 44-proof spirit, which would burn quite nicely at 76 degrees, tastes like gin mixed with Brussels sprouts and anise. Drink it to say that you drank it, in anticipation of saying that you didn't like it and never want to drink it again.

PLAY ALONG AT HOME

The game 421 is played with three dice and a dice tray. When it's your turn, you get three chances to roll a 4, 2, and 1. If you roll any of those numbers on your first try, you pick that die up and place it on the rail of the dice tray. The same on the second roll. If, after the third roll, you have a 421, the other person must buy you a beer. It requires absolutely no skill and is based purely on luck. But it's quite addicting.

A Belgian Drinking Game

Want to drink like a Belgian? Play like one. Back in 1910, Theophile Vossen ran the bar called La Cour Royale. Many of its customers, working at the National Bank of Belgium, would come to the bar on their lunch break and play a game called 421. In the last round before returning to their office (to crunch numbers with a nice buzz), the loser was called *morte subite*, which translates literally into "sudden death."

When Theophile moved his location to its current address in 1928, he took the name Morte Subite for his bar. While that's not the most inviting name for a bar, or a brand of beer, it's a necessary stop for any beery day of activity in Brussels. I met up with "Bart the Bartender," the chain-smoking, poodle-toting bartender, to "learn about beer," or in our case "drink about beer." They offer a good selection of Belgian beers, as well as their house gueuze beers, which are mighty tasty. Now, as a seasoned traveler, I love reading menus that have been translated into English. Usually Chinese restaurants provide the best fodder for humor. But at Morte Subite they would like you to note that "besides our drinks, we propose you degustations, sandwiches and various omelets." Good to know.

In the course of drinking, I also learned that Bart will happily take

a beer as gratuity from a customer, in lieu of money. Whenever I'd bartended, I'd always helped myself to as much beer as I wanted. If someone tipped me

with a beer, it would be like buying apples from a fruit vendor and giving him one of his own apples as a tip. But in Bart's case, and in a country that doesn't tip as consistently as we do in the United States, he was happy to accept liquid compensation, and upwards of twenty of them in any given day. Even I thought that sounded like a lot . . .

Bart: Oh, it's nothing, twenty beers. I start working at ten in the morning and I finish at two in the night [morning]. So, I work for fifteen, sixteen hours.

Zane: You're really telling me that you could drink twenty beers in a day? And then afterward you go out and have a beer to relax . . . ?

Bart: Yeah, because when I finish the job, because we have a lot of stress—

Zane: Well, I don't know how stressed-out you can be by drinking all day . . .

Bart: We have a lot of stress . . . And when I finish my job, I like to breathe. And I like to be relaxed. And I go to a bar which is still open in the night and I have five, six beers . . .

The Next Morning

As much as Brussels offers religious experiences for beeries, it offers the same prize for foodies. One theory about hangovers is that stuffing your face, especially with unhealthy comfort foods, will alleviate your hangover. In Belgium, a food coma is the perfect way to avoid feeling the effects of your ale hangover.

Grab some mussels and fries, topped off with a generous splash of vinegar. I recommend Café Leon, where they serve up half a ton of mussels a day (so you can be sure your food is always fresh). If you're looking for authenticity, it should be noted that french fries were invented in Belgium, so *moules frites* (the local way to ask for mussels and fries) are extra appropriate. And if you're looking for a dish that doesn't require utensils, you've also come to the right place. As I learned, in Belgium you don't need a fork or a spoon—you just use the emptied shell as a pincer to capture your mussels. And for a little hair of the dog, try the house beer, with orange essence. Yum.

Remedy rating: *Two out of Three Sheets. A food coma (followed by a nap) often does the trick.*

Chapter 5
Poland

Latitude: 52°00' N

Longitude: 20°00' E

What they call it: Polska

What they speak: Polish

How to say cheers: *Na zdrowie!* (To your health!),
Do dna! (To the bottom!)

Hangover remedy: Pickle soup

Poland (PO-lund) 1. A former communist member of Russia's Eastern Bloc. 2. A major player in the Vodka Belt. 3. A place where they are as serious about their vodka as they are about their pickles.

There are a few tricks to getting along well in Poland. The first is an ability to sound out very long words. With provinces like Swietokrzyskie, Wielkopolskie, and my personal favorite, Zachodniopomorskie, you can see how that would be a useful skill for getting around. The second is an enduring appreciation for the potato. The potato in Poland is as ubiquitous as Starbucks in America—which is to say, it's everywhere, and hard to avoid if you're looking for a snack or a drink. You'll find it in potato pierogis, potato pancakes, and—my personal favorite—potato vodka.

People in Poland really like their vodka. While I was there, some folks told me that "Po szklanie i na rusztowanie" is a favored saying of Polish construction workers, meaning "Another glass and we'll go onto the scaffold!" And according to my source, they weren't talking about water. Which brings us to rule number three for surviving in Poland: Avoid construction sites!

Not Just for Holding Up Pants!

Poland is smack dab in the middle of Europe's Vodka Belt. From Oslo to Moscow, of all of the Vodka Belt countries, Poland may be the most significant.

Vodka has had a long time to embed itself into the national consciousness. While it was likely around much earlier than the sixteenth century, according to documents, vodka has been made in Poland since the 1500s, when it was used mostly for medicinal purposes. But it came with many side effects, including hangovers, streaking, late-night pierogi parties, and weepy conversations with the ex.

The Vodka Belt is an unofficial string of countries that have a long history of producing good vodka. They are Finland, Norway, Iceland, Greenland, Sweden, Denmark, Estonia, Latvia, Lithuania, Poland, Belarus, Russia, and Ukraine.

Today, there are literally hundreds of brands of Polish vodkas on the market, although only a handful of them are imported to the United States. This was just one of the positive effects of the fall of the Iron Curtain. Personal freedom was another. With the privatization of distilleries, a bevy of new brands came onto the market. In the days of communism, after World War II, all of the distilleries were "taken off the hands" of their owners by the new communist government. During that time, the Polish government rationed vodka as they did bread or shoes.

Under communist rule in Poland, vodka was produced by Polmos, a state-run monopoly. Polmos is an acronym for "Poland Spirit Monopoly." Call it like it is.

Vodka 101

Vodka is commonly defined as a "neutral, colorless, near-flavorless distilled spirit." Vodkas have been made from ingredients ranging from potatoes and grains to fruits and even milk. The area of contention in the Vodka Belt is that, by definition, anything that is distilled to a high percentage of alcohol will be clear, colorless, and near-flavorless. They would like vodka to be limited to its original ingredients of potatoes and grains, maintaining an appellation of its own. But, in some interpretations of the definition, whiskey, tequila, rum, and brandy distilled to the point that they fall under the guidelines of the definition are "essentially" vodka. Many companies have taken it upon themselves to create vodka with what is regionally available, such as Pau Maui Vodka, made in Hawaii from pineapples. After all, what would you call a "neutral, colorless, near-flavorless distilled spirit" made from pineapples? It's a debate that the European Union has attempted to quell by requiring vodkas sold in the EU to specify their ingredients on the bottle. But that would be like requiring major league baseball players who use steroids to wear an S on their chests. What would that accomplish?

Nowadays recognized as one of the most popular spirits in the world, vodka was generally absent from American liquor cabinets until the 1950s. But by 1975 it had surpassed bourbon as the most consumed liquor in the country. Its popularity is attributed to its not having as strong a smell or taste as other spirits on the market. Eventually it even replaced gin as the top ingredient for a martini. What also made it popular was its "mixability." Because of its subtle taste, it was easily combined into a wealth of new cocktails, such as the Moscow Mule, popularized by the vodka brand Smirnoff in the 1940s when it wanted to make a splash in the American alcohol market.

HOW TO MAKE A VODKA MARTINI

As vodka became more popular in the United States, the fashionable gin martini gave way to the vodka martini, sometimes served dirty, with olive brine added, and sometimes garnished with a lemon twist.

One chilled cocktail glass

Two ounces of vodka

Half an ounce of dry vermouth

Pour over ice in a cocktail shaker, shake, and pour into your chilled cocktail glass. Garnish with an olive or a lemon twist. For a dirty martini, add a quarter ounce of the salty brine that your olives are swimming in to your cocktail shaker along with the spirits.

HOW TO MAKE A MOSCOW MULE

One part vodka

One part lime juice

Three parts ginger beer or ginger ale

Mix together and pour over ice.

Wodka 101

In Polish, *woda* means water—and *wodka,* little water, is the diminutive. But as any vodka drinker knows, a *little water* can go a very *long way* . . .

Polish vodka is usually 80 proof. While in other places people might substitute grapes or apples for the hardworking potato/grain spirit ingredients, serious vodka makers in the Vodka Belt believe that in order for a spirit to be considered "vodka," it should be distilled from a mash of potatoes or grain.

One of these people is Tad Dorta, whom you can consider the Donald Trump of vodka: He is one of the key figures responsible for vodka's inclusion in the luxury spirit market today. Remember back in the 1990s, when all we really knew of vodka was Smirnoff and Absolut (because of those clever magazine ads)? Today, of course, there are dozens of options in every bar, each more costly than the next. Dorta is the dude who is personally responsible for that phenomenon. When the communists buggered off in 1989, Tad saw the potential for capitalizing on a product that had previously been under strict government control. So he founded two vodka companies, Chopin and Belvedere, to appeal to the world market of liquor. He literally created the premium and luxury vodka market.

Chopin was the first vodka to be packaged in a frosted wine bottle with a clear window, revealing the magnified image of Polish composer Frédéric Chopin on the back of the bottle. Now there are so many frosted bottles that it has become the accepted way to present a luxury vodka.

Like other purists, Tad believes that true vodka is made strictly from potatoes and grains. He also feels that vodka is best served at room temperature. The very popular chilled vodka loses flavor and texture, with the lower temperatures killing some of the taste and thickening the liquid. To Tad, being able to taste the subtlety of the potatoes or grain is an important part of the vodka experience.

Because of the low freezing point of alcohol, vodka can be stored in ice or a freezer without any crystallization of water. But don't tell Tad I told you!

The Vodka War was not a bar fight, but an event in 2006 when several Vodka Belt distillers requested that the European Union reserve the term *vodka* for spirits distilled with traditional ingredients such as potatoes or grains. In the end, the EU did not prohibit distillers from making vodka from nontraditional ingredients, but it did require that those ingredients be indicated on the bottle.

VODKA: BEYOND POTATOES

Vodka brand	Distilled from
Grey Goose	Wheat
Pau Maui	Pineapples
Vermont White	Milk!
3 Vodka	Soy
Ciroc	Grapes
Triple Eight	Corn
Eden	Apples

FILTER THIS

Vodka ignorance has caused some to get caught up in the number of distillations and filtrations that a vodka goes through. Logically speaking, if five distillations truly produced a more superior vodka than distilling it three or four times, everyone would distill their vodka five times. Or why not six? Or ten? Or a hundred? That's because each time a vodka (or any spirit) is distilled, it loses some of its tastes and characteristics. A potato vodka that has only been distilled once has a more earthy taste, with the distinct smell and taste of a potato (a little "earthy," which is a nice way of saying a little "dirty"). But by distilling it four times and letting it go thought several filtrations, the final product is smoother and more "neutral" and only retains some of the subtle characteristics of the potato.

Wodka 102: Taste a Rainbow of Flavor

Many traditional vodkas have additives to essentially give them flavor, and sometimes color. And I'm not talking about a cosmopolitan, dirty martini, or fruit flavors. Most of the recipes are hundreds of years old and their flavors reflect their environments.

In contrast to the citrus flavors added to many of the popular vodkas, traditional Polish vodkas are flavored with locally harvested wild grasses, flowers, roots, and herbs, giving the final product a distinct taste of the region.

One of the most popular flavored vodkas is Zubrówka (zhuh-BROOV-kah), which has been made in Poland, near the Lithuanian border, since the 1500s. It gets its taste by being steeped with bison grass. But don't go looking for it at your local liquor store. While you may find a replicated product, the original version, while still popular in Poland, is banned in the United States. In 1978, the U.S. Food and

MORE FLAVORED VODKAS

Flavored vodka	Pronounced	Flavored with/from
Dziegielówka	dieo-gloof-ka	Lavender, angelica, and oregano flower
Debowa	dao-bo-va	Black elder flowers; matured in oak
Imbirowa	eem-beer-ofka	Floral herbs and ginger
Klosówka	kla-sav-kal	Oregano and rye husk
Krzeska	ker-shes-ka	Cloves

Drug Administration outlawed its sale because it contained coumarin (usually found in fragrances), which is considered a toxin.

Zubrówka contains a signature single blade of grass in each bottle. And while the bottle of Zubrówka that you may find in a specialty liquor store looks the same, down to the decorative blade of grass in the bottle, and tastes very similar, it's a coumarin-free version.

Fire and Sword

Warsaw may be the capital of Poland today, but Krakow claims a long and varied history that traces back to the Stone Age, when Prince Krakus, who killed the dragon that lived in local caves, founded the city. And while the city is known for its universities, culture, and art, I will remember it for two drinking experiences: one that I loved, and one that I'm in no rush to do again.

First I visited a restaurant, Ogniem i Mieczem, whose name translates into "fire and sword." They serve up some amazing meat, and an amazing drink called Miodula. Miodula is a blend of rye vodka, secret herbs, and honey vodka that is filtered and then aged in oak barrels. Because of the distilled rye, aged in oak, it tasted like Scotch with a touch of honey. It's one of my favorite spirits.

There's Gold in Them Waters

At the Alchemia Bar, they do something very special with Goldwasser (GOLD-vah-ser). I use the term *special* very loosely.

Goldwasser is an 80-proof vodka product that is flavored with roots and herbs native to the town of Danzig. The most notable quality of the spirit is the flecks of real gold floating in the bottle. (You may be familiar with the more popular Goldschlager, a cinnamon schnapps from Italy that also has gold flakes in the bottle.)

If you've ever thought about collecting a bunch of bottles and siphoning out the gold (oh, I'm the only one who's thought that?!), it may not be worth your time. Each bottle contains one-tenth of a gram of gold, which was worth roughly three dollars at the time of my writing this.

When Goldwasser, invented in 1598 by Ambrosius Vermöllen, was first developed, gold was thought have beneficial medicinal qualities. That might not have been the case, but something else proved more important: It was an ingenious marketing ploy. Goldwasser became popular with leaders and nobility, possibly because of the assumption by spectators that they have so much money they can drink it (in the form of gold flakes) and not even bat an eyelash.

There's nothing wrong with Goldwasser, but I still take exception to the way it was served to me in Krakow. The bartender heated up a snifter of Goldwasser and lit it on fire. He then poured the liquid into another glass, capped the snifter with a bar coaster, poked a hole in it, and had me inhale the vapors. It burned. Supposedly, this gets it into your bloodstream more quickly. Suffice it to say, that was not the problem. Suffice it to say, I did not ask for a refill. Suffice it to say, I didn't hold it against the spirit—just the bartender.

What the Folks Drink

In order to learn more about the folk liquors that have been made privately for generations, I met with a bunch of young people in a bar. I heard that people who came from families who distilled the stuff would be sharing their secrets; they heard that a guy who loved to drink was coming. I thought I'd be learning, and they thought I'd be getting hammered.

Mateuse, who spoke the best English, explained the rules of a drinking game that he had learned from his grandfather. It was developed by soldiers right after World War II, when the troops were still deployed but were just sitting in the trenches, bored to death.

A board was brought out that had seventy-one squares on it. Each player got a shot glass to use as a playing piece, which was advanced along the board according to their roll of the two dice. At your turn, you'd roll the dice, move your glass along, and do whatever was asked of you when you landed on your spot.

The commands on the spaces ranged from "everybody drink" or "everybody except for the roller drink" or "all of the men drink" to more arcane tasks like "saw a log in under a minute," "hold an 18-kilo [40-pound] log with your arms parallel to the ground for five seconds," and "hammer a 10-inch nail into a log in nine or less blows."

The drinking commands were pretty straightforward, but the tasks carried a reward of three shots of vodka if you were successful or seven (yes, seven) shots of vodka if you failed your task. After a couple of rolls and a number of shots, I started to do the math . . . With five of us playing, and the average roll of dice being seven, there would have been a minimum of fifty opportunities for each of us to drink. So I decided to call a tie after only a few turns, and declare all of us winners, so I could learn about some of Poland's folk liquors rather than just pounding them and forgetting what country, or planet, I was in.

Sliwowica (shlee-vo-VEET-sah), also called plum brandy, or plum vodka, has traditionally been a homemade product, although it's also commercially available. It's usually fairly strong. I was offered a shot from a bottle of 190 proof (95 percent alcohol). After I took the shot, it took a few moments for it to burn, which it did. I then chased it with a bottle of water. Historically, it's been used as medicine. But I can't figure out why something so strong is still sold. It's basically un-

drinkable. It's so strong that it has been used in the field to clean the wounds of soldiers (probably after they've had a healthy swig).

In the old days, when a child was born, the proud father would make a barrel of Starka, seal it with beeswax, and then bury it in the ground. On the day that child got married, the barrel would be exhumed and consumed.

Starka is a Polish (and sometimes Lithuanian) vodka made from rye and aged in oak barrels. It can be aged anywhere from five to fifty years. It's essentially very similar to whiskeys distilled from rye and then aged in oak barrels. Even the color is similar, due to the time it spends in oak. Starka, however, is traditionally steeped with lime blossoms or apple leaves.

Krupnik (KROOP-nik) is a grain-based alcohol sweetened with honey. It's considered a liqueur by many, even though it should technically be called liquor, as it's at least 80 proof and can be as high as 100. There are countless recipes for Krupnik, since, as a privately produced spirit, its recipe was passed down through families. The basic recipe for Krupnik is grain alcohol infused with honey, but dozens of different herbs can be added.

LIQUOR VS. LIQUEUR The delineation between
liquor and liqueur is not as clear as a line drawn in the sand. While it mostly
refers to the alcohol content, there is no benchmark for when liquor becomes
liqueur. Liquor is defined as a distilled beverage. Liqueurs usually have sugar
and flavoring added to them, and have an alcohol content of less than 30 percent.
But the addition of flavor or even sugar does not automatically make liquor a liqueur.
Liqueurs were created when liquor was thought to have medicinal benefits,
but tasted too bad to force down the gullet. While my grandmother
may not have gotten the memo ("Zane, get Nana her medicine—
it's in the bottle from a man named Jack Daniel"), liqueurs
are now served as cordials, or, more often, mixed
with other ingredients to make cocktails.
Liquor, on the other hand, is still considered
medicine in some circles.

HOW TO MAKE PEPPER VODKA

Really, don't make this. Seriously, why would you want to?

Boil water.

Add pepper.

Pour into a bowl and mix with a generous amount of vodka.

Add additional sprinkling of pepper.

Consume, or better yet, convince someone else to try it.

Pepper Vodka

Unlike Absolut Peppar, which has a subtle peppery taste that works
perfectly in a Bloody Mary, a Polish folk version of pepper vodka that

Mateuse introduced me to was anything but subtle. It was vile. Half of the credit for that goes to the ingredients; the other credit goes to the drunken maker. I'll drink anything once, but some things I will never have twice. His recipe is above.

A Wedding in Wisla

Two hours outside of Krakow, near the border of Slovakia and the Czech Republic, is the town of Wisla, a beautifully forested summer retreat. But I wasn't there for the hiking, the scenic views, or the castles—I was invited to "observe" the drinking rituals at a wedding.

I had already been warned that the Polish typically drink more vodka at weddings than any other occasion throughout the year. To give you an example, the wedding I attended had 130 guests (including me). The bride and groom had considered all factors—and brought 150 bottles of vodka to the reception. This is an even more impressive number when you consider that Polish women typically do not drink vodka. So they brought thirty bottles of wine in case the women also got thirsty. Oh, and some beer. And they planned to consume it all.

The cousin of the bride spent the day walking around with a basket full of ice-cold bottles of vodka. Along with enough supplies to keep the tables well stocked, he had an open bottle and a stemmed shot glass. If you crossed his path, you would be offered a shot—and by offered, I mean *very* strongly encouraged. You were not asked, you were told. And it was tough to refuse. After his fifth visit to our table, I deduced that in Polish, "No" means "Please pour me an overflowing shot of vodka and then stand there emphatically shouting at me in Polish until I give in and drink it."

It was at the wedding that I met Arthur, who offered to share some Polish drinking customs with me. Arthur had a sly look, and as

---

MAKE BOTTLE EASY OPEN

How to open a bottle of Polish vodka like you were born in Zachodniopo-morskie.

Pick up a bottle of Polish vodka that has never been opened. Turn it upside down and smack the bottom of the bottle with your arm, just above your elbow.

Twist the cap.

See, wasn't that easier? No? Me neither.

---

soon as I put my hand on the cap, he asked if I knew how to properly open a bottle of Polish vodka. I let go and sat back for a demonstration.

He smacked the bottom of the bottle like a bad baby in the '50s. I asked why. But after much deliberation, even the old-timers at the table had no better answer than "Make bottle easy open." Maybe some things don't need to be any more complicated than that.

At some point in my vodka tutelage, I asked the bride and groom how long the wedding reception would go. I was wondering how quickly I could sneak back to my hotel, because I had to be up early the next morning. My survival instinct was kicking in.

Zane (casually): The reception started at four, right?
Groom: Yes, and we will go all night.
Zane: Until when, midnight?
Groom: Until the morning.
Zane: How late? Like, until three?
(As they laugh, I am relieved, assuming I have overshot my estimation.)
Groom: Like, seven.
Bride: Eight.

Groom: Eight ... (And he'd only been married for a few hours. Gooood husband.)

Soon after this conversation, as I tried to dance my way toward the door, the groom offered to give me a break from vodka. So he brought me a beer ... with a surprise.

Nuremberg: Location of the Postwar Tribunals? Not Today!

Of course, it wasn't just a beer—what would be the fun in that? It was a "Nuremberg," a large, icy beer (about half a liter) with a full shot of vodka dropped into it. Every country has its own version of the beer bomb. Now I was faced with Poland's.

To get an edge in a chugging contest, make sure your beer isn't too cold. If you have no control of that, then without being obvious, hold the cup or glass with both hands to warm it up. Every degree makes a difference. The more you know ...

HOW TO MAKE A NUREMBERG

The Polish beer bomb, no questions asked.

Fill a large pilsner glass full with Zywiec (a light lager).

Drop in a chilled shot of your favorite Polish vodka.

Chug.

In Poland, they love their vodka, but they also love their beer. The favored locally produced beers come from the Zywiec, Okosim, and Lomzar breweries.

Poland makes up the   tenth-biggest beer market in the world, and when you compare them to the rest of Europe, they slide in at number five. That means that no matter how much vodka they drink, beer is the preferred chaser. And appetizer. Or, in the case of my Nuremberg, a cocktail mixer.

Polish Party of Beer-Lovers (PPPP; Polska Partia Przyjaciół Piwa) is an actual political party in Poland that was started by Janusz Rewinski, a Polish actor, activist, and satirist.

POLAND: YEARLY LIBATION CONSUMPTION, PER CAPITA

Vodka	5.7 liters
Beer	95 liters
Milk	173 liters

I placed it to my lips, tilted it back, and poured it down my gullet. I could feel my throat going numb from the chilled liquid. I could also feel about a hundred sets of eyeballs watching me to see if I could finish it in one fell swoop, which is, of course, the only way to properly finish a beer bomb in any country.

Just as my eyes began to water up, I saw the bottom of the glass. A few more gulps, one tremendous belch, and I had two empty glasses in my triumphant fist—the one that held the beer, and the one inside it that held a heaping shot of vodka.

In a Fine Pickle

After a day and night of debauchery at the wedding of people I barely knew—but who quickly felt like family, especially after I stumbled out without saying goodbye—I woke up feeling as if I'd spent a day at a tribunal keg party. I needed something salty, something soothing, something that I had never even dreamed existed: I needed pickle soup.

Pickle soup is made from pickles, cream, potatoes (of course), dill, broth, and *genius*. Really, it's like heaven in a bowl. Hot, salty, delicious, unexpected (that's what she said) . . . let's just say it isn't a terrible way to wake up in the morning, especially when you've just come from a party where the vodka-to-person ration is more than one to one.

Remedy rating: *Two out of Three Sheets. It didn't cancel out the effects of an evening capped off with a Nuremberg, but it was a hearty soup that hit the spot.*

The Americas

While people lived in the Americas long before the Europeans got there, the arrival of the "civilized" world brought distillation techniques to the native populations, helping turn the local preference for fermented agave into the drink that we know today as tequila. In fact, the European drinking influence is apparent all over the Americas and the Caribbean. Argentines love their Italian aperitifs and digestifs and their best-known grape is a French import. St. Martin is still owned by France and Holland. Jamaicans are inordinately fond of Guinness. And Vegas, of course, has its very own Venetian canal.

Chapter 6

Tequila, Mexico

Latitude: 45°26' N

Longitude: 12°19' E

What they call it: Tequila

What they speak: Spanish

How to say cheers: *Salud!* (Health!)

Hangover remedy: Drowned sandwich

Tequila (tuh-KEE-luh) 1. A region in the Mexican state of Jalisco (ha-LEESE-co). 2. A distilled beverage made in the Tequila region. 3. A spirit that I've sworn to never drink again…on several occasions.

Mexico is a country renowned for its beaches, Mayan temples, and drinks with salted rims served poolside. Most tourists' knowledge of drinking in Mexico comes from spring break or a family vacation at some beach resort filled with, well, other tourists. But those all-inclusive resorts, border towns, or even hustling Mexico City are a far cry from what most of Mexico is like. To get a feel for the real Mexico, you gotta go inside the country, outside the wristbands-required resort, and away from the big hotels. And, as delicious as they are, you'll have to put down that frozen drink with the cute umbrella if you want to play along.

What You Should Drink in Mexico...

Mexico has some great lagers, such as Corona, Dos Equis, Pacifico, Modelo, and a bunch of others. They also have a burgeoning wine industry, making, among several varieties, some nice cabernet sauvignons. But the alcoholic libation that Mexico is best known for, and deservedly so, is tequila, a spirit made from the blue agave plant.

Mention tequila and many people will respond with a shudder of horror or a long-winded story about fleeting love, the spotty recollection of an altercation, or a raging hangover. But despite the world's obsession with pairing a shot of tequila with a shake of salt on your wrist and chasing it with a bite of lime, in much of Mexico tequila is meant to be revered, not gulped.

Fine tequila is like a cognac. It's made with passion and meant to be sipped and experienced. And, like cognac, it has a region in its country dedicated to it.

...and Where You Should Drink It

Like the United States, Mexico is divided into states. Jalisco, one of its thirty-one states, reaches inland from the Pacific Ocean. There are a few noteworthy items about Jalisco. 1. The capital of Jalisco, Guadalajara, is the second-largest city in Mexico (after Mexico City). 2. Puerto Vallarta, a city in Jalisco, is one of the most popular tourist destinations on the west coast (after Acapulco). 3. Most important for our purposes is a small town a few miles northwest of Guadalajara that was established in 1874. The name of that town is Tequila.

A private, nonprofit group called the Consejo Regulador del Tequila (Tequila Regulatory Council) enforces, with the blessing of the Mexican government, the regulations that control the quality and production of tequila. They ensure that the official classifications for tequila are being abided by and maintained.

Tequila lies in the shadow of the Volcán de Tequila, or "Tequila Volcano." The volcano last erupted two hundred thousand years ago, and when it did, it left behind a rich volcanic soil perfectly suited for growing the main ingredient in tequila: agave.

TEQUILA TRAIN

If you visit Tequila, you'll most likely stay overnight in the city of Guadalajara and make a day trip out of visiting the distilleries. A great way to do this is on the Tequila Train, a fiesta on rails. It departs from Guadalajara and makes the ninety-minute trip to the town of Amatitan, in the Tequila region, while passing small villages along the way. There's a bar in every car of the train, along with mariachis and other music. Upon arrival in Amatitan, you will have a full day of authentic Mexican food and tequila. Let's just say the trip home will be quieter than the trip there. Siesta!

The Mexican government enforces the designation of their national spirit as coming from a specific region and created under a set of strict guidelines. Just as champagne can only be produced in specific areas of the Champagne region of France, tequila can only be produced in specific areas in the Tequila region of Mexico.

The History of Tequila

Long before the first margarita was mixed, the natives of what is now Mexico were making a fermented, not distilled, beverage from the blue agave plant. As it is with maple trees, the agave were tapped to remove the sap without having to destroy the plant. The

The agave plant is not a cactus, but is actually a member of the lily family.

aguamiel, or honey water of the starchy blue agave, could then be fermented into a kind of agave wine. This drink was called pulque.

Tequila was first officially imported into the United States in 1873. Today we consume more than a million cases a year.

When the Spanish conquistadors arrived in Mexico around 1520, they brought, along with their destructive tendencies and Christianity, distillation technology that could produce a more potent potable. European distillation met New World ingredients, and tequila, essentially the first spirit of the Americas, was born.

The first person ever issued a license to manufacture tequila, by the king of Spain, in 1758, was a man by the name of José Cuervo (which translates into English as "Joe Crow"). His company started with a small parcel of land and quickly became the largest producer of tequila, which it still is today. Herradura and Sauza started in the 1800s.

HOW TO MAKE A MARGARITA

Sure, you can buy a mix and just add tequila. But why would you do that when it's so easy to make one that tastes so much better?

1½ shots of 100 percent agave tequila

½ shot of Cointreau

1 shot of fresh-sqeezed lime juice

Glass rimmed with salt

Mix the ingredients and pour over ice. *Olé!*

As it did for Canadian whisky, America's Prohibition did wonders for tequila's popularity. Its popularity was also helped by World War II, when getting booze from overseas became difficult. Oh, and the invention of the margarita didn't hurt. Recipes for this popular tequila cocktail first appeared in American magazines in the early 1950s, and we've been drinking them steadily ever since.

How Agave Becomes a Hangover

When the early pulque drinkers made their favorite spirit, they did so without harming the agave plant. Today this is not the case. There are more than 300 million agave plants harvested for tequila every year—and none of them survive. Good thing they're happy to sacrifice themselves for the cause, because it takes fifteen to twenty pounds of agave pulp to make one liter of tequila.

Here's how it works: The blue agave plant (*Agave azul tequilana weber*) is covered in giant, spiny, dusty blue-green leaves, called *pincas*. When the agave are ready to be harvested, at about eight to twelve years, the *jimadors* (the people who harvest the agave) remove the pincas until they are left with the heart of the plant, called a *piña,* which is Spanish for "pineapple," because it looks just like a giant white pineapple. The piña is covered in a multitude of tiny fibers, like fiberglass, which can burn if they come into contact with your skin—a lesson that I learned most painfully.

In case you were planning on planting and harvesting an agave yourself, at home, you should know that there is no mass-produced tool for the removal of pincas from a piña. The jimadors are forced to make their own, often from the leaf springs of cars, which they flatten and sharpen until they can slice off a pinca without even applying much pressure.

If you have an agave that seems about the right age for harvesting, you'll definitely want to consult a jimador, whose job it is to determine when the agave is good to go. An immature plant won't be starchy enough to produce enough sugar for distillation. A plant that is too ripe will grow a stem that resem-

Oak barrels are often charred, which gives the tequila its smoky flavor. Some companies use new barrels, but many buy used whiskey barrels from the United States. The used barrels even impart some of the tastes of their previous tenants.

bles a giant asparagus right before it dies. And when I say giant, I mean gigantic. These agave stems can grow to be forty feet tall, after which the agave scatters its seeds to the wind and goes straight to agave heaven.

The piñas that the jimadors have cleaned up weigh around fifty pounds each. These are loaded into trucks and brought to the distillery, where they are chopped in half and placed in giant ovens that steam them, converting the starches to the necessary sugars. Steamed agave piña tastes a bit like grape jelly (in *my* opinion).

The cooked, sweet piñas are then shredded and juiced. The juice is put into fermenting tanks, where yeast is added. For about two days, the yeast eats up the sugar, pooping out alcohol. The fermented mixture is then distilled into tequila and aged in oak barrels for anywhere from never to years and years.

The Five Basic Types of Tequila

If you want to be able to identify types of tequila by sight, you're in luck: Color has a lot do with it. Tequila, like Scotch and other spirits, gets better with age.

Blanco, which translates into "white," is also called "silver" tequila. These tequilas, whether 100 percent agave or not, are un-aged and never see the inside of an oak barrel. They are therefore clear and have no coloration. These are the "entry-level" tequilas, although some are considered quite good. They provide the most authentic taste of the distilled agave, since no other flavors (like oak) are introduced. Blanco tequilas are diluted (to 35–55 percent alcohol) and bottled right after distillation.

Oro, or "gold" tequila, is also called *joven* (young) tequila. The best example of this is the bestselling tequila in the United States, Cuervo Gold. It's neither a blanco, because it's gold in color, nor a reposado, because it's not aged. Gold tequila is a *mixto* of silver tequila with the addition of caramel for color and flavor. Because of the additional ingredients, it's never 100 percent blue agave tequila. It's most popular in margaritas, because with the addition of sugar, ice, and lime juice, you wouldn't taste the nuances of a more complex (and more expensive) tequila anyway.

Resposado, or "rested" tequila, spends anywhere from two months to a year sitting in white oak casks or barrels. This chill-out time mellows the tequila slightly and gives it a peppery or oaky taste. It also gives the reposado its pale golden color. It takes on the flavor of the barrel, but doesn't spend enough time there to mellow out as much as the añejo. It is considered smoother than blanco tequila.

Añejo, or "aged" tequila, must spend a minimum of one year in oak barrels. This gives it time to take on some of the characteristics of the oak, while also mellowing. But if aging it for a year or two makes it great, wouldn't aging it for fifteen years make it amazing? The reason that it's not aged for longer is that the more you age it, the more you are replacing the subtle flavors of the agave with the overbearing flavors of the barrel.

Ultra-premium and reserva, expensive options for tequila, have recently become more popular. An ultra-premium is aged for over three years, while a reserva is distilled for up to eight years. A reserva is worth trying. It tastes similar to aged Scotch or cognac, but because of the hot climate, it ages more quickly, picking up a lot of the flavors of the barrel and becoming as mellow as a whiskey or brandy twice its age.

One Tequila, Two Tequila

Many tequila makers would like to think that tequila has reached the status of brandy and cognac, often sipped and enjoyed over deep conversation. However, that day has not come...yet. But while tequila may not yet be seen as "refined" by mainstream America, it is certainly on its way. We don't generally savor tequila as we would an old Scotch, but tequila bars have opened up in major cities, and as more expensive ultra-premium and reserva brands have come onto the market, tequila isn't just for banditos and spring breakers anymore.

Before you start to sip, you must know what you are sipping, and why.

Whether a bottle is a blanco or an añejo, there is still an additional distinction that lets you know which should be savored and which is begging to be mixed with lime and sugar. There are two

---

HOW TO MAKE A BLOODY MARIA

Much like a Bloody Mary, but with tequila instead of vodka.

One part tequila

Two parts tomato juice

Enough of your favorite hot sauce to make your mouth burn

Enough lemon to make your mouth pucker

Top it off with celery salt.

kinds of tequila, based not on age or color but basic ingredients. All tequila must be between 70 and 110 proof (35–55 percent alcohol). But some are made from agave and some from 100 percent blue agave, a distinction that must always be noted on the label.

Agave tequila: Regular tequila is mixto, a mixture of 51 percent blue agave juice and 49 percent other sugars. It can be exported in bulk to

---

HOW TO MAKE SANGRITA

Sangrita, or "little blood," is a completely different drink from sangria (a fruit and wine mixture from Spain). It is traditionally served in a tall shot glass next to an equally tall shot glass of tequila. Serve a slice of lime in a third glass . . . fancy! This three-glass serving style is commonly known as a bandera, or "flag," in honor of its resemblance to the red, white, and green flag of Mexico.

1 cup tomato juice

⅓ cup of lime juice or 3 limes, squeezed

⅓ cup of orange juice or 3 small oranges, squeezed

Hot sauce or minced fresh green jalapenos to taste

Salt and pepper

Combine all ingredients and mix well. Serve bandera style.

---

be bottled in other countries, as long as they abide by the tequila regulations. An example of this is Cuervo Gold, the most common brand in the United States. These tequilas are best used in mixed drinks, such as margaritas or Bloody Marias.

100 percent agave tequila: This high-quality spirit is made with 100 percent blue agave juice. It's designated on the bottle as 100 percent agave tequila. It must be bottled at the distillery in Mexico. These are more expensive, and considered to be higher quality than regular tequila. This is the kind of tequila you'd like to sip, perhaps accompanied by some homemade *sangrita* . . .

Mescal

Of course, there's more than one way to cook a piña. While tequila is a spirit that must be made specifically from the blue agave plant, and in designated areas of Jalisco, mescal is a spirit made by baking the agave piña in a charcoal pit, giving the resultant distillation a smoky flavor. Tequila can only be made from one agave variety, while mescal can be made from any of five different types of agave. And it should be noted that mescal is often distilled only once, which retains more of its original flavor than tequila, which is generally distilled at least twice.

Technically, all tequila is mescal, but mescal is not always tequila. Still, it shouldn't be seen as an inferior product—it's just different. While there are over five hundred kinds of tequila, there are only about one hundred brands of mescal.

Tequila aficionados will tell you that worms are found in bottles of mescal, while mescal lovers will tell you that the worm is a myth.

Mescal has nothing to do with mescaline. They aren't even cousins. Mescaline, also known as 3,4,5-trimethoxyphenethylamine, is found in peyote, a type of cactus, and is a psychedelic alkaloid. As mentioned, agave isn't even a member of the cactus family—it's a lily.

Remember: Mescal can make you drunk, while mescaline can make you think you're a cactus.

EXCUSE ME, SEÑOR, BUT
THERE'S NO WORM IN MY DRINK

Bottles of tequila often contain a worm.

Nope, not true. Bottles of tequila never contain a worm. It would break the rules of being called tequila, because the worm would be considered an ingredient. And knowing how strict the Tequila Council is, that would never fly, even as a gimmick.

Bottles of mescal often contain a worm.

Not exactly. Bottles of mescal rarely contain worms. But they sometimes contain a pickled worm that is purely a marketing ploy.

Question: If that's the case, then why have I seen bottles with a worm in them?
Answer: It's a pickled worm.
Question: Does that make it less gross?
Answer: Not really.

There are no psychotropic or hallucinogenic effects that come with eating the worm, and it is not a proven aphrodisiac. At least, nothing happened to me.

Drown Your Hangover

In Guadalajara, the most popular remedy for *el crudo* (a hangover) is a sandwich called *torta ahogado* (drowned sandwich). It comes loaded with meat, to which you layer on your own toppings, including generous amounts of hot sauce, thereby drowning your breakfast—and your hangover—with extra spice. According to researchers (both academic and those engaged in fieldwork), food that is spicy, high in fat, and high in protein serves to distract you from being hungover, so you focus on the fact that your mouth is on fire instead of your tequila-fueled headache. Spicy food can actually *increase* your hangover. A component of a hangover is dehydration. By sweating from spicy foods, you are essentially dehydrating your body even further.

Remedy rating: *Three out of Three Sheets. Despite my increasing dehydration, I also enjoyed a few beers. Not exactly hair of the dog (you're loco if you think I'm having tequila for breakfast). But the filling sandwich and spicy sauce did the trick.*

Chapter 7
Argentina

Latitude: 34°00' S

Longitude: 64°00' W

What they call it: Argentina

What they speak: Spanish

How to say cheers: *Salud!*

Hangover remedy: Yerba maté

Argentina (ar-jen-TEE-nuh) 1. The second-largest country in South America, after Brazil. 2. Home of Ushuaia, the southernmost city in the world. 3. A place where the grapes are from France, the liquor is from Italy, and the universal language is from Spain.

Argentina and its neighbor to the west, Chile, occupy the southernmost point of South America. *Argentina* means "land of silver," and while the cities are totally first-class, it's still a place where cowboys roam the plains. Of course, the cowboys are called gauchos and the plains are called pampas. But there are a lot of cows, which is good, because Argentines like their beef as much as they like their booze. They are serious about their barbecue, and they are serious about their wine. When I was there, I ate a lot of meat prepared outdoors, gaucho-style. And I learned a lot about wine, specifically Malbec, the region's favored grape. But I also drank some other things . . .

The Paris of South America

The capital of Argentina, and its biggest city, is Buenos Aires. It is renowned for its restaurants, nightlife, and architecture, and is sprinkled with wide plazas where people can hang out, just like in Europe, which is part of why Buenos Aires is known as the "Paris of South America." But Argentinean culture has taken its cues from all across Europe, melding together the Spanish, French, Italian, and native influences.

The city is full of life and culture, past and present, from sky-scrapers to old, intricate buildings. It's a place where you can learn to tango, go to the opera—or go a different route, and instead just drink everything the city has to offer, like the most popular drink in town, an Italian import that is also an Argentinean favorite.

Proud to Be Bitter

I met up with reps from Fernet-Branca at a café in Plaza Dorrego, one of the city's many outdoor squares. We cracked open a bottle of fernet and they explained to me how it all went down.

Fernet is an *amaro*, which means "bitter" in Italian. It's an herbal liquor from Italy that is traditionally served at the end of a meal as a digestif, a beverage that will supposedly help you digest your meal. There are many types of fernet, but they too contain spices, herbs, roots, and fruits, such as juniper, anise, lemon peel, fennel, licorice, cinnamon, cardamom, and saffron. You can also add them to coffee or espresso, or use them instead of bitters in cocktails.

People who live in the port city of Buenos Aires are known as *porteños*, which means...people who live in a port city...brilliant!

Fernet-Branca is a specific kind of fernet that was invented by Bernardino Branca in 1845. The ingredients are mysterious, mostly because they are kept secret by the company. I kept asking but the reps wouldn't tell me what was in it. But I'm betting they probably just didn't know. All they would tell me was that the flavor was "complex." I say it tasted like "spicy prune with peppers." It's definitely an acquired taste. At first I didn't care much for it, but the locals surely do. Since then I've had it on several occasions. I've gone from "hated it" to "didn't mind it" to "that wasn't so bad" to "well, I guess

I'll have another if you're having another." I'm working my way up to "like it."

It may be bitter, but the people at Fernet-Branca are proud of that. It's part of the company's marketing campaign. Since it was brought to Argentina by Italian immigrants, Fernet-Branca has become a national favorite. I didn't just hear it from the reps, who are paid to say it: Fernet with cola is the national cocktail.

Today, fernet is only manufactured in two places: Italy and, only as of recently, Argentina.

> Fernet and Coke even has a song written about it ... "Fernet con Coca," by Vilma Palma.

HOW TO MAKE FERNET AND COLA

The favored drink in Buenos Aires and across Argentina. It may be an acquired taste, but what's wrong with a little acquisition?

One part fernet (from Italy)

Four parts cola (from the United States)

Pour over ice (from Argentina!).

Drink.

A Spoonful of Sugar

Right across from Plaza Dorrego is Todo Mundo, a bar that serves a Gancia Batido, another popular cocktail in Buenos Aires. The Gancia Batido is made with Gancia Americano, a vermouth made from sparkling wine and then flavored. The Gancia company harks way back to 1850, when Carlo Gancia used French winemaking methods he picked up in Reims and brought home with him to Italy.

Argentines typically head out for the evening around ten or eleven and stay out until four. At least, that was what I saw happening around me. And how did these revelers keep themselves up so late? The daily siesta, a nice nap after lunch when it's extra hot out, doesn't hurt.

Like fernet, it's an Italian import made with herbs and spices, has been around for a long time, and is definitely an acquired taste. Unlike fernet, which is a digestif meant to be taken *after* a meal, Gancia is an aperitif, meant to be enjoyed *before* a meal. This 14.8 percent alcohol sparkling wine vermouth is not as bitter and dry as martini vermouth.

HOW TO MAKE A GANCIA BATIDO

I wasn't a fan of this one. Even with the sugar added, it still didn't go down so easily. But everyone around me seemed to think it was delicious. So, maybe I just needed some more time, or more knowledge . . .

Gancia Americano

Squeeze of lemon

Spoonful of sugar

Shake vigorously.

Serve over ice.

The favored beer in Argentina is Quilmes; the company owns 75 percent of the Argentine beer market.

There are two distinctions with alcohol when it comes to taste. Some taste good right off the bat, and some take some getting used to. I remember thinking my first beer tasted like carbonated urine. But I kept drinking them, and now I can't get enough of the stuff. Jägermeister is a similar story, although I never "need" a shot of Jäger. But I certainly appreciate it more now than when I first tried it. For whiskey, it was the same thing—although I'm sure my first whiskey was the cheapest available. I didn't know what I should have expected in the taste, and was therefore surprised with what I got. I've come to realize that appreciation comes with knowledge. Knowing the history, ingredients, and process that went into creating Fernet-Branca or a Gancia Batido makes it easier to appreciate. Plus, when I have one now, no matter where I am, I'm transported back to the night when I first tried them in Argentina.

Mendoza

Wine is an alcoholic beverage that is usually made from grapes. Duh? Well, technically speaking, though, any beverage made from fermenting fruit would be considered wine. All that's needed is the addition of yeast, and the fermentation process can begin.

Wine, as we typically know it, made with grapes, has been made by humans for the purpose of consumption for around eight thousand years, starting in Mesopotamia. (Egypt didn't get in on the action for another three thousand years.)

The countries that produce the most wine, by volume, are France, Italy, Spain, the United States, and, in fifth place, Argentina. Number six is China, which will probably surpass everyone by 2020 (in more than just wine production, if they have their say).

The yeast organism has been around since the Cretaceous period and has thus been taking advantage of fallen fruit for longer than humans have been around to consume it.

It makes sense that the Europeans are so gung-ho about wine production—for around two hundred years, during the fourteenth and fifteenth centuries, clean drinking water was scarce and so wine (and beer) became a part of the daily diet.

The most significant wine region in Argentina is Mendoza. It has some of the world's worst drivers, and some of world's best wines (I'm hoping those facts are unrelated). You can hop a quick flight from Buenos Aires to Mendoza to visit the wineries. But if you want to stop by all of the wineries, it may take a while. If you want to hit one a day, it'll take you around two years, because there are some seven hundred wineries in and around Mendoza.

> The only alcoholic beverage older than wine is beer, which people have been enjoying for around ten thousand years.

The most significant wine grape in the most significant wine region of the fifth-highest-producing wine country in the world is the Malbec, which makes for a rich, spicy, and delicious accompaniment to a meal (or anytime, really).

All Grapes Are Not Created Equal

The Malbec grape emigrated from France to Argentina in 1868 alongside Michel Pouget, an architectural engineer. It's a red grape that hails from the area near Bordeaux, where it grows mainly in the Cahors region. In France, it's one of the six grapes that may be used in making a Bordeaux, and it is appreciated mostly as a blending grape, as opposed to one that is made into a wine on its own.

The Malbec grapes in Argentina, which are grown mostly in Mendoza, are distinct from the ones grown in France. This is likely a com-

The first vines were planted in Mendoza more than four hundred years ago. When the Spanish conquistadors arrived in Argentina, in Mendoza, instead of a dry desert they discovered a system of irrigation being used by the local tribe, the Huarpes. This suggests that the area may earlier have been a southern stomping ground of the once mighty and ferocious Inca. Today's irrigation system still uses those same channels (updated and improved, obviously), giving wine growers in the region a specific edge in grape growing. Too much rain is a problem for grapes. According to Argentinean winemaker Jacques Lurton, "If it rains on ripe grapes for more than a week, some serious problems such as botrytis may show up, leading to rot and loss of color." The lack of rainfall plus a sophisticated irrigation system means that during hot desert days and cool desert nights, they completely control the water supply, allowing for a sweeter and more intensely flavored grape.

It takes more than half a pound of grapes to make a glass of wine (five ounces)—for a bottle, nearly three pounds.

bination of the difference in terroirs and the phyloxera epidemic of the late nineteenth century, which may have killed off any trace of the granddaddy of all Argentinean Malbecs, the specific strain of Malbec that was originally brought over from France.

In fact, in France, the Malbec's use has been in decline as other grapes have risen into favor. In Argentina, the Malbec's popularity has been on the rise for several decades. It has been embraced as the national wine of Argentina, and like the country, it's a wine that is definitely learning to hold its own on the world stage.

The Wine Thief

A wine "thief" is a tube that you stick in the bunghole (that's what he said!) to steal a taste of wine from a barrel. The vintner (winemaker) typically spot-checks barrels to keep track of each batch's development. It's not a completely passive process, as the vintner may have to decide whether to mix young wine with different varietals or grapes from other years before bottling.

The Malbec grape needs more sun and heat than a cabernet sauvignon or a merlot grape to mature, which is exactly what Mendoza gives it.

WHAT A DIFFERENCE A LITTLE TERROIR MAKES

	Cahors, France	Mendoza, Argentina
Where		
What	French Malbec (Côt Noir)	Argentinean Malbec
Terroir Factor #1	Maritime climate	Higher altitude
Terroir Factor #2	Sandy, iron-rich soil	Direct sun
Terroir Factor #3	High humidity	Low humidity
Result	Intense flavors	Softer and richer flavors
Use	Used mostly in blends	Single grape wine

If you find yourself before an array of bottles, here's how to manage the tasting order so as not to overwhelm your delicate little taste-buds.

First sparkling, then white, then red.

Drink the youngest wines before the older wines.

Light wines should precede heavier wines.

Dry always goes before sweet.

Cheap before expensive, also known as "Box before bottle."

But not until the wines are mature do they taste like "wine." Before the yeast has done all of its work, the batch tastes like carbonated grape juice, which is low in alcohol. According to the vintner, we weren't tasting for a finished product, but rather checking the young wine for color and density of body. He also explained that Malbec from Mendoza is 14 percent alcohol, stronger than wine from other regions, because of the power of the sun. Thanks to *el sol*, which shines in Mendoza around 320 days each year, the fruit develops more sugar—and sweeter fruit means a higher alcohol content.

How It Goes Down at a Vineyard

Vineyards differ in size, focus, and production, but the process at each remains generally the same. After the grapes ripen, the vintner tastes the grapes that have grown over the hot summer season and determines how sweet they are and when they should be harvested. In Argentina, since they are in a different hemisphere than the United States and Europe, the grapes would be harvested in late March or April.

Once the vintner decides

Many vineyards are surrounded by olive trees. Why? Do they protect the vines from wind? Yeah. But mostly it's because they grow in similar climates and produce an additional marketable crop.

> Date
>
> A green harvest is a process of removing immature grapes from the vines. By removing a good deal of the grapes, the theory is, the vines will continue to work as hard for the remaining grapes as they did when the vines were full. This makes the surviving grapes more robust and flavorful but decreases the yield of grapes, and wine, that the vineyard produces. The green harvest is usually done with fine (more expensive) wines.

that it's time to harvest, it's all systems go. The employees of the vineyard hustle to harvest the season's grapes as quickly as they can once the winemaker has declared the sweetness to be pitch perfect. The grapes that have been picked are shuttled to the winery in big bins. Upon arrival, they are mercilessly crushed.

If the winery is making white wine, they will remove the skins and the seeds to prevent the resulting product from taking on any extra color. If they're after red wine, the skins and seeds remain to give the wine its rich, deep hues.

The crushed grapes are then transferred to stainless-steel tankers that are sometimes big enough for a grown man to have a nice dip in (but unfortunately, not this man). The grape juice gets a helping of yeast from the vintner, and as the yeast begins to digest the sugars (remember all that blazing, brilliant sunshine?) it leaves alcohol behind as a most intoxicating waste product. One yeast's garbage is another man's magic potion...

A Proper Tasting

After a day spent at the vineyards, I headed back to Mendoza for a proper tasting, just to round off my day of wines. I had spent the day saturating myself in red wine culture. Now it was time to taste some mature wine.

I visited the Vines of Mendoza tasting room and talked with Ariana, a tasting coach who was happy to line up a row of glasses and match me, sip for sip (after a little encouragement). We tried a Torrontes, a wine that is considered to be 100 percent Argentinean. If Malbec is their favorite import, Torrontes, which is only produced in Argentina, is their favorite local. If Malbec is the red wine of Argentina, Torrontes is its white.

Torrontes is about the same color as chardonnay. Ariana explained that as white wines age, they get darker. (The color of a white wine can also be improved by aging it in an oak barrel.)

We tried the Torrontes according to the five S's of wine tasting. First we looked to *see* what color it was. Then, in order to properly appreciate the nose, or aroma, of

THE FIVE S'S

1. See
2. Swirl
3. Smell
4. Sip
5. Savor

Ever wish you had your own vineyard? Vines of Mendoza wishes the same thing. Anyone with money can buy a vineyard, and the company will tend the vines and help you develop and brand your own wine.

the wine, we *swirled* it to release the flavory goodness. Then we *smelled* it. Finally, we *sipped* it and then *savored* it.

White wine should be served chilled but not too chilled—aim for 60–68 degrees Fahrenheit.

Ariana asked me what the wine tasted like, and I'll admit that I wasn't sure. I mean, it tasted like wine. So she helped me out a bit. She put some other stuff in various glasses and had me give them the sniff test. There was a glass with ginger, a glass with honey, and a glass with green apples. The "compare and contrast" method helped a lot. Also, it was a lot like cheating—she basically gave me the answers. But Ariana was right—the Torrontes did have notes of apple, honey, and ginger. I guess that's why she has her job. But here's why I have mine—because the next day, I got to head to an area sixty miles south of Mendoza, at the base of the Andes mountain range, where Ariana's boss, Pablo, played *asador*, offering me a mountain of meat and another glass of wine, this time a spicy Malbec.

Asado, Gaucho-Style

Barbecue in Argentina has a three-hundred-year history. Back in the 1800s, instead of a grill, you would have seen a *parisia*, a smoldering pit with a cow over it. Today, Argentines are a little more genteel—but just as committed to their meat. The *asador* is the grill master; he usually would have been a gaucho. As Pablo explained, gauchos have three hundred years of experience finding the right cows to eat.

We ate and drank with the Andes hovering in the background. Delicacies presented from the *asado* are often presented in a specific order. I wasn't really paying attention, though—I was just shoveling all of the carnivorous goodness into my face. Asado offerings can include chorizo, black pudding, *mollejas* or sweetbread, *asado de tira* or ribs, flank steak, chicken, and sometimes a baby goat. One popular sauce is *chimichurri;* it's a delicious green preparation of parsley, oregano, garlic, olive oil, and other flavorings.

If you are on Weight Watchers, are a vegetarian, or are planning on traveling with a baby goat, this may not be the best country to visit. Otherwise, come quickly. There's a piece of meat on the grill with your name on it.

Resaca Remedy

Obviously, this is an easy place to drink too much, and eat too much. So while in other places a hearty breakfast might seem like the perfect antidote, in Argentina, when my *resaca* (hangover) hit, I longed for something a little less filling. In Argentina, the popular hangover remedy is yerba maté. Pablo introduced me to this tea, a member of the holly family.

Drinking the maté tea, which is brewed from the leaves, is a serious ritual in Argentina. People sip this stuff all day long. It's got some caffeine but it's lighter than coffee.

Remedy rating: *Two out of Three Sheets. It wasn't the miracle I'd been promised. I was so hoping that it was this amazing hangover cure that I could introduce to everyone back home and, well, make a fortune on. But it was just okay. Back to workin' for a livin', I guess.*

Chapter 8
Jamaica

Latitude: 18°15' N

Longitude: 77°30' W

What they call it: Jamaica

What they speak: English and Jamaican patois

How to say cheers: Cheers!

Hangover remedy: "Herbal" tea

JAMAICA, MON

Negril

Appleton Estates

Kingston

Jamaica (juh-MAY-kuh) 1. An island of the West Indies in the Caribbean Sea. 2. Birthplace of Bob Marley and reggae music. 3. North America's leading exporter of ganja.

Just south of Cuba is an island where you can go. And should. Some people love Jamaica for the sun, the sand, and the hair braiders who will make you look like Bo Derek (or Kevin Federline, depending on your generation) for a few dollars, but I prefer to keep my focus on the five R's: rum, Red Stripe, reggae, Rastas, and reefer.

So after getting settled in my hotel in Negril, on the western-most part of the island, I ventured inland to find my first R.

Yo-Ho-Ho and a Bottle of R

Before Columbus landed on Jamaica, before the development of all-inclusive resorts with dance clubs called "Jamaican Me Crazy," the island was the home of a group of Arawakan Indians called the Taino. In their language, the island was "Yamaye," the land of springs. In fact, Jamaica's bountiful spring water is one of the integral ingredients for one of my favorite things to drink there . . . rum.

Jamaica's oldest distillery, the Appleton Estate, in St. Elizabeth's Parish, is named after its founder, James Appleton. According to available documentation, Appleton Estate has been making rum in Jamaica since 1749. But according to legend, it was already in business

Nineteen sixty-two was a magical year for Jamaica. Not only did Jamaica finally claim her independence from Britain, but that very same year, Sean Connery made his debut as British spy James Bond in Dr. No—which was shot in Jamaica. Coincidence? I bloody well think not. English writer Ian Fleming, who penned the James Bond novels, was actually a resident of Jamaica, not England. There's a beach named after his most famous character, called Octopussy Beach. (Actually that was a dumb joke for Bond nerds; it's called James Bond Beach.)

when England took control of the island in 1655. When the English began shipping the rum back to England it became very popular. And while the long, arduous journey back home couldn't have been much fun for the sailors (you ever have a hangover at sea?), it had an added benefit for the rum: The time the full barrels spent rocking in the waves further smoothed and mellowed the rum, making it a tasty as well as intoxicating export.

Since Appleton Estate gets most of the ingredients for their rum right there on the property, the production of their rum has always been almost entirely self-contained. Sugarcane grows on the property and is processed into sugar at the estate's own refinery. The convenient by-product of the sugar refining process? Molasses. Appleton ferments their homemade by-product with yeast, which grows on the same sugarcane, mixed with water from natural springs located on the estate (the Taino weren't just being creative when they named their island: Jamaica is full of volcanic and mineral springs). Then the mixture is distilled. The result: God's gift to pineapple and coconut juice.

As it finishes the distillation process, rum is crystal clear and quite high in its alcohol percentage. It's then brought down to a more "drinkable" alcohol content with local spring water, and then aged in the barrels. Like any aged spirit or wine, rum develops some subtle flavor notes over time. The aging mellows the rum (brings down the alcohol percentage) and brings out some of its natural flavors, but most of the distinct flavors are a result of contact with the charred oak barrels.

Appleton currently ages its rum in oak barrels that were once used to age American bourbon (the barrels are the only "ingredient" that don't come from the estate). In fact, when sipping one of Appleton's premium rums straight, you should be able to pick up the slight taste and smell of bourbon.

APPLETON ESTATE'S RUM

Product	Aging process (in bourbon barrels)	The bouquet and flavor notes (according to Joy)
Appleton White	Aged then charcoal filtered	Coconut, pear
Appleton Special	Aged in oak barrels and blended	Vanilla, ginger, nutmeg
Appleton Estate V/X	Aged up to 10 years	Orange peel, "spices"
Appleton Estate Reserve	Aged 10–12 years	Orange peel
Appleton Estate Extra	Aged 12–18 years	Coffee, coconuts
Appleton Estate 21	Aged 21–30 years	Rich vanilla, coffee, hazelnut, almond

I was lucky enough to get a prep course in rum with Appleton's master blender, Joy, who at the time was, and may still be, the only female master blender in the rum business. She explained that the aging greatly affects the flavor of the rum. The longer the rum sits in the barrels, the darker the color and the richer the flavor. To illustrate this, and to help me fully appreciate what makes Appleton so distinct, she took me through the Appleton Estate rum "ladder."

After sipping some of their best rums, Joy and I made our way over to the Appleton Estate Rum Bar to sample some rum concoctions. As the bartender whipped me up a rum punch, Joy watched from a distance. I sipped the punch, made with Appleton's white rum, and concluded that if it tasted this good with a young rum, it would most definitely taste great with an older rum.[1] So, I grabbed the bottle of twenty-one-year-old Appleton Rum and began making a rum punch. Joy, watching from the wings, was aghast.

A local bartender shared some folklore about Appleton in the old days. Apparently, during Prohibition, it was illegal to sell Appleton Estate rum that contained too much alcohol—today's levels would have been completely unacceptable. Still, tastes haven't changed that much, and old-timers liked their higher-proof rum as much as we do today. Since the potent stuff was very popular with the patrons, the bartenders always kept a bottle of the higher proof hidden under the bar. When someone wanted a stiffer drink, instead of requesting the banned Appleton rum, they'd order a glass of "bend down," because the bartender had to bend down to get the bottle.

[1] I would like to point out that at this point I had not yet gotten the education that I received from shooting in Tequila, Kentucky, Scotland, Cognac, or homes of the various other spirits that are aged in barrels. Therefore, I did not appreciate the subtle nuances that are achieved by letting a spirit soak in wood for over a quarter of a century.

Joy: You took my most expensive rum and put it in a cocktail!

Zane: But I . . .

Joy: Big mistake. Big, big, big mistake!

Zane: Lemme ask you a question . . . If this [the Appleton X/O] is good in a mixed drink, why is this [the twenty-one-year-old] not awesome in a mixed drink?

Joy: Because . . .

Zane: Because, why? [I'm embarrassed to say that, at the time, I really didn't get it.] I don't understand.

Joy: Because this rum is an ultra-premium rum that you should just sip.

HOW TO MAKE RUM PUNCH

There are countless recipes for rum punch. Generally it's a combination of rum and punch. (Duh!) I visited Walkers Wood, a spice company in Jamaica's St. Ann's Parish (the area where Bob Marley was born), and they suggested this recipe.

1 cup fresh lime juice

2 cups brown sugar

3 cups Appleton rum

4 cups various fruit juices (orange, pineapple, guava, etc.)

Shake and serve over ice with a dash of Angostura bitters, fresh ground nutmeg, a slice of lime, and a cherry.

Depending on how sweet the fruit juices are, you might want to cut back on the brown sugar. My mother recommends that you experiment with a new recipe before throwing a party. Or you can do as I do, and experiment as an excuse to throw a party.

> **Zane:** Okay . . . [Still wasn't sinking in]
>
> **Joy:** Do you know how much that bottle costs?
>
> **Zane:** How much is it?
>
> **Joy:** It's going to go for one hundred and fifty dollars U.S. next time it's on the market.
>
> **Zane:** I didn't know that . . . [as she walks away, I take a sip of my "expensive" punch]. By the way—it tastes awesome . . .

It sure tasted good, but Joy was right: It was too complex in flavors for the punch. Since then, I'm pleased to say, I have learned from my mistake and have never done anything like that again (at least, not with rum). Clearly you, the reader, would *never* do something like that, so I'm sure you have nothing to learn from my experience.

Rastas

Contrary to the belief of college kids everywhere, Rastafarianism is not about growing dreadlocks, getting stoned, and downloading Bob Marley's *Legend*. Sure, the stereotype of a chill Rasta with a big spliff isn't totally off-base, but real Rastafarianism is a religion with many devout followers. It emerged in the 1920s and '30s in Jamaica and is widely believed to have begun with the teachings of the famous writer, philosopher, and activist Marcus Garvey, who preached a form of pan-African loyalty.

According to tradition, Garvey predicted that a black king would rise to power as the savior of people of African descent, no matter where they lived; his teachings were very popular among disaffected African Jamaicans. Around the same time, 7,668 miles away, Haile Selassie was crowned "Ras Tafari," emperor of Ethiopia. Selassie said that he was a direct descendant of King Solomon, which meant that he was King of Kings, the Lion of Judah. There were many Jamaicans who saw him as a prophet and savior and viewed his rise to power as an awakening for Africans around the world.

This is, of course, a book about drinking, and while a devout Rastafarian wouldn't typically endorse drinking, there's a reason that I included it in my five essential R's. Not only is it a big part of Jamaican culture, but I enjoyed (if enjoyed is really the right word) one of my most local drinking experiences on the island because one self-proclaimed "Rasta Mon" thought that there was a drink that was a must-try.

At Three Dives Jerk Shack in Negril, I was enjoying the best chicken of my life (sorry, Mom). The slow-cooked poultry was crispy on the outside while moist and delicious on the inside. As I devoured my meal, I was joined by a guy (names avoided to protect the guilty) who seemed to breathe smoke instead of oxygen and insisted that there was a drink that I couldn't leave without trying. If I gave him twenty bucks, he said, he'd go down to the market and grab us a bottle to share. After the legal but seemingly illegal transaction, he returned with a brown paper bag containing our distillate, a bottle of overproof JB rum. (Incidentally, because it "cost exactly twenty dollars," there was no change.)

JB, which is manufactured by Appleton, is an acronym for John Crow Batty rum, the official name of the brew. Some feel the name refers to the smell of the contents, because they stink like crow—although I highly doubt a rum company would think it was good marketing to name a rum because it smells like a dirty bird. Locals call the drink "vultures." It may be because if you drink enough, you're likely to pass out and be consumed by vultures. Seriously, this stuff was strong. Overproof rum is rum that is too high in proof to meet exportation standards. It is not aged, and never even sees an oak barrel. In many cases it's not even reduced in alcohol percentage with water. In the case of JB "overproof," the alcohol content was 63 percent (126 proof).

While a very good reason to drink alcohol is for the effects, most of us seek out drinks that also taste good to us. Some choose deliciously made liquors and sip them straight; others are grateful to the cranberry bogs and lemon trees for making cocktails even more tasty. Most alcohols are made in such a way as to make them more palatable. JB is not one of those.

I poured a shot into the cap, although my new friend took a break between inhales to recommend mixing it with Pepsi. But I wanted to get the taste and experience of it without cutting it with a sugar-laden soda. The rum tastes like an alternative fuel source for my car with a slight, *slight* taste of vanilla. It burned. There is only one reason to drink it—to get Steve McKenna'd.

As I shook the Rasta-mon's hand and thanked him for his time, he led me around the back of the building, to the cliff overlooking the beautiful blue water. There he handed me a "hand-made cigarette." "I'm okay," I told him. But he wouldn't take no for an answer. And since it's rude to refuse a gift, I accepted it (in exchange for the ten-dollar donation he requested after I accepted the gift). As he went back to finish the chicken plate that I bought him, carrying his ten-dollar donation, my change from the JB, and the rest of the bottle, I still walked away a winner. I had another amazing experience—and a joint to share with my friends back at the hotel (not that they would ever indulge in such a thing).

Red Stripe

The third *R* is for Red Stripe beer. In Jamaica, wherever you find beer, you'll find Red Stripe. In fact, wherever you cast your eyes, you'll find evidence of Red Stripe—their billboards, posters, and coasters cover just about every possible surface, and every tourist drinks it. I sure did. I've been to Jamaica several times, and bought enough Red Stripe to put a kid through private kindergarten. But was I really getting the "authentic Jamaican experience" that I intended? Maybe not. While the short, round Red Stripe bottles (the Danny DeVito of drinking vessels) are plentiful, and the lager really does hit the spot on a typically hot Jamaican day, I soon learned that it is, in fact, not what the locals generally prefer.

Reggae

Reggae is truly the music of the island, and Bob Marley is without a doubt the most well-known figure to ever come out of Jamaica. "I Shot the Sheriff" can still be heard booming out of car stereos and floating out of old radios sitting on windowsills. Many, many bands have tried to fill the shoes of the godfather of reggae, and everywhere that you go in Jamaica, you will see them trying.

One evening, I was invited to check out a reggae band warming up for that night's performance. They let me dance around onstage like an idiot, so everyone watching *Three Sheets* could see how "spontaneous and crazy" I am . . . Afterward, I offered to buy them a few rounds. They happily accepted. I asked the bartender for a dozen Red Stripes, which, as discussed, is what most visitors to the island assume is the most widely quaffed beer. Widely, perhaps, but locally . . . not necessarily. All of the musicians whose drinking I sponsored that afternoon changed their order to Guinness.

Zane: But why?
Reggae band member: [Shrug.]

Well, there you go . . .

I was aware that Guinness, the most successful beer brand in the world, is brewed in many countries other than Ireland, but I never considered that it was a "warm weather" beer. Nothing beats a rich and creamy pint of the dark stuff on a dreary day in Ireland. But on a hot and balmy day in Jamaica? Apparently so. So I switched my order to stout and drank what the other guys were drinking. Truth be told, I prefer Red Stripe, or any cool lager, on a hot day. Get me in Ireland on a typically cool day and offer me a draft, I'll pick Guinness every time.

Bottles, which is how most of the Guinness on the island is consumed, are not nitrogen-pressurized, which causes the beer to be creamy, so it was definitely a different experience than the creamy Guinness from the tap (or Guinness from one of those cans with the nitrogen capsule).

During Prohibition in the United States, a Jamaican ginger extract containing 70–80 percent ethanol, usually marketed as a medicinal extract, became a popular alternative to illegal alcohols. It became known across the United States as "Jake." Friendly name, not such friendly consequences. When the extract became illegal under Prohibition, some amateur bootleggers modified the recipe and sold it on the black market. Unfortunately, the new form of Jake hurt a lot worse than a hangover. The liquid contained a neurotoxin that caused paralysis in frequent imbibers, usually in the hands and feet, resulting in a strange gait. Such paralysis came to be known as Jake foot or Jake walk. Today, in Brooklyn, you can visit the JakeWalk Bar on Smith Street and enjoy a "Jakewalk" or a "Jakeleg" cocktail (with a headache as your only potential repercussion).

The Guinness bottling plant and the Red Stripe plant, interestingly, are one and the same. Desnoes & Geddes Limited, producers of Red Stripe, was originally formed in 1918 as a soft drink company (you can thank them for beverages like Ting grapefruit soda). They eventually opened the Surrey Brewery in Kingston and introduced an ale, but when the locals deemed it too heavy, they switched to a lighter lager, which is what Red Stripe is today. In 1993, Guinness acquired a controlling interesting in D&G. In addition to Red Stripe and Guinness, they also produce Dragon Stout, which, oddly enough, tastes very similar to Guinness—especially in the bottle.

Herbal Remedy

For a hangover remedy in Jamaica, I was presented with a cup of tea. But it was not like any herbal tea I'd ever drank before. It was in a cup, sure, and it was definitely relaxing, but it wasn't chamomile or Earl Grey. Specifically, it was marijuana, cannabis, Mary Jane, herb, ganja, reefer, grass, pot, cheeba, bud, Buddha, sinsemilla, or wacky tobaccy. But it wasn't in a bong. It was on the *menu*. Like Bill Clinton, "I did not inhale." I did, however eat and drink it.

I was greeted at Ted's Tea Shack by Ted himself. It's no surprise that he didn't send a representative to meet with me because his is a one-man operation. His "shack" is also his home, which has a kitchen, living room, bedroom, and bathroom and occupies about 250 square feet, total. Ted's a warm, very down-to-earth guy who genuinely welcomed me into his home. He showed me around (which didn't take long) and brought me back to his kitchen. There he fired up his small stove and, as he brought some water to a boil, offered me a piece of cake, which was more like a brownie, but without the cocoa. I ate and we talked about business.

I asked Ted how he operates his Tea Shack without worrying about the law. Despite the fact that, in Jamaica, pot is easier to get than cigarettes, bottled water, or a sandwich (I mean, I didn't walk along the beach that morning and have seventeen people come up to me and offer to sell me a ham and cheese, Marlboros, and an Evian), possession of marijuana is against the law in Jamaica. Yes, just about every bartender, bellboy, or taxi driver can get you a dime bag in less time than it takes you to check in to your hotel—but that doesn't mean you can't get in trouble for it, unless, like Ted, you "know people." Ted explained that if the cops were to show up, he'd have "plenty of time to tidy up."

There have been many discussions in the Jamaican government about legalizing or at least decriminalizing ganja. But Jamaica receives millions of dollars in aid from the United Kingdom and the United States, and if Jamaica were to legalize marijuana, it would likely be violating the 1988 antidrug policy set forth by the United

Nations, and thereby make it unlikely that they would receive any foreign aid, except maybe from Amsterdam. And the United States doesn't really want them legalizing pot. If it were legalized, things could get even stickier for U.S. customs officials, considering that Jamaica is *already* the leading exporter of Mary Jane to the United States (something they'd like to nip in the bud).

But just because the officials aren't *haters* doesn't mean that they're *players:* Don't think that this apparent lax approach means you can walk the streets puffing on grass. Jails all around the Caribbean are clogged with people serving time for various ganja-related offenses.

But that's enough talk about the law. It's teatime.

When the water came to a boil, Ted threw in four giant buds, and then he reduced the tea to a simmer. (For a stronger effect, adding some whole milk to the mixture helps coax the THC out of the leaves.) After letting it steep for a bit, he led me to a table under a giant palm tree. There he put two unmatched teacups on the table and covered them with a small cloth towel that he used to strain the tea. A drop of local honey for flavor, and we were ready to drink. To my surprise, it tasted like marijuana—I know, what did I expect? And it was probably the worst-tasting tea I'd ever had. Less to my surprise, after fifteen minutes I was starting to feel very relaxed.

Zane: I'm starting to feel really relaxed.

Ted: Ya, mon.

Zane: I'm stoned.

Ted: No, not yet.

Zane: Really?

Ted: Not for another fifteen, twenty minutes.

And he was right. I was drinking tea with a mellow cat in Jamaica—of course I was relaxed. But I wasn't stoned. Pot that is eaten or drunk in a liquid takes longer to get into your system. But when it does . . . wow.

About thirty minutes later, I and my crew packed up, said our thank-yous to Ted, and were on our way. As we often shoot the show out of consecutive order, we still had one thing on the agenda. It was about one-thirty in the afternoon when I went to go chill at the hotel, assuming I'd be right as rain by the time the driver came back for me at four. Can you guess where this is going? "Nowhere" would be the correct answer. When they called me at quarter of four, I was still stoned—even more than when they had left me. So, I didn't make it to the last location. In fact, I'm pretty sure I was still stoned the next morning as I made my way to the airport.

Grandma didn't make tea like this!

Remedy rating: *Four out of Three Sheets. Did I feel hungover? Shit, I couldn't even feel my legs!*

Chapter 9

St. Martin/
St. Maarten

Latitude: 17°59' N

Longitude: 63°10' W

What they call it: St. Martin/St. Maarten

What they speak: English, French, and Dutch

How to say cheers: Cheers! (English), *Santé!* (French), *Proost!* (Dutch)

Hangover remedy: Fresh coconut water and gin

St. Martin (MAR-tin) or **St. Maarten** (MAHR-tn)
1. An island in the Caribbean. 2. The smallest landmass
in the world that is divided between two nations
(France and the Netherlands). 3. Home of the "erection
tree." (Seriously, you can't make this stuff up.)

Two halves make a whole, and that's how it is on St. Maarten/St. Martin. The Dutch side, being a holding of the Netherlands, is spelled *St. (Sint) Maarten,* and the French side is spelled *St. Martin.* The island doesn't feel as schizophrenic as it sounds, even though neither half of the island constitutes a country on its own. Since the two halves have peacefully coexisted since they literally drew a line in the sand in the 1600s, as a traveler all you have to do is sit back and enjoy.

Good Fences Make Good Neighbors

According to folklore, the split was not unlike siblings deciding to draw a line of masking tape across a bedroom to delineate who owns what. When the border was purportedly disputed, a Frenchman and a Dutchman were selected to walk across the island. The Frenchman, drinking wine, and the Dutchman, drinking beer, each walked as far as he could around the island in an effort to claim territory for his side. The spot where they met marked the border.

It must have been some walk, because while the island isn't as big as, say, Jamaica, it's definitely not so small that you could walk around it in a day. Unless you were in very good shape. Its circumference is about thirty-seven square miles, with marshes, beaches, tributaries, bays, and rocky coastlines. But who am I to question a good story—especially one that makes alcohol sound like a sports drink?

Dutch St. Maarten

Flying into the island will most likely land you at Princess Juliana Airport on the Dutch side. After collecting your luggage, take a break from the mini-bottles of booze you threw back on the plane and pop into the Sunset Beach Bar for a full-sized libation. Don't worry about looking funny dragging your luggage down the road . . . the draw of the Sunset Beach Bar is not really the drinks, the sunsets, or even the fact that topless women drink for free, but rather its proximity to the airport. The bar is literally at the front of the runway. You might also note that the runway is short enough that large jets need every inch of it to take off and land, so the planes come so close to Sunset Beach that they've been know to clip the fence with their wheels or, as was the case when I was there, blow out the windows of cars parked in their path.

While you're sitting on the picnic tables with your luggage piled next to you, watching the planes land and listening to the tower chat with the

inbound planes on the barely audible speaker, which is clipped above a surfboard that has flight times scribbled on it with chalk, ask the bartender for a Carib beer. Like most beverages on St. Martin, Carib is not made on the island. It's a lager made in Trinidad and Tobago, St. Kitts and Nevis, and Grenada. The company started making the beer in 1961, and, according to their website, they dropped $60 million to compete on the world stage (it was in Trinidad dollars, not American dollars, so it was only around $10 million U.S.). It tastes like—beer. Which after a long flight and a walk down a dusty tarmac, hits the spot.

Before grabbing your bag and heading to your hotel, I wouldn't suggest standing in the jet wash of the planes that are about to take

off. They have a limited amount of runway to work with, so the takeoff strategy is to lock the brakes and gun the throttle before hurtling down the runway (think slingshot). This kicks out a sustained wind of 60 mph (up to 80 mph from the 747s), which makes standing in one place difficult, and strangely fun. I held my ground in the jet wash as a layer of my skin was eroded by the sand and a seagull was temporarily pinned against the fence. I already mentioned the car windows, but honestly, it bears repeating. (Please keep in mind that this is reportage, not a recommendation.)

Two Countries, One Bar

If you're having a tough time deciding on which side of the island to have your next drink, avoid the hassle. Visit the Dinghy, a bar built over Oyster Pond. The pond is not actually a pond, but a saltwater cove with a marina. It's the first bar I've found that spans two territories. You enter through French St. Martin, sit at the bar in Dutch St. Maarten, and use the urinal in French St. Martin. How continental!

Owned by a Frenchman named Matt and his American wife, Cara, the Dinghy has a relaxed, easy atmosphere and feels like a neighborhood tavern (if your local tavern has no walls, warm ocean breezes

The Arawak Indians, the original inhabitants of the island (they settled Jamaica, too—great taste in real estate, the Arawaks) called it Sualouiga, which means "Land of Salt," because of the lack of fresh water. Even today, the entire island uses desalinated water. It tastes fine, but you might want to substitute bottles for your water needs—bottles of Carib, that is! Ba-dum-dum ching!

All of the island's twelve casinos are on the Dutch side.

year-round, and overlooks a marina). The bar is largely unremarkable, filled with sailors passing through and a smattering of locals. What *is* remarkable, however, is their generous happy-hour special.

They say that their happy hour is here to stay. But every business

The port of St. Maarten is a favorite stopping-off point for cruise ships. Every year, 1.4 million blue-haired nanas and walker-toting grampas cruise through to Philipsburg, the capital of Dutch St. Maarten, an irresistable destination for duty-free enthusiasts and tchotchke hoarders.

model that I've worked up concludes that they'll be out of business in less than seven months. Anywhere else, when you order a drink, you call the booze and the mixer. But here, after you order up a rum and Coke, the bartender will give you a large glass with ice, a bottle of Mount Gay rum (not made on the island), and a can of cola. It's then up to you, the customer, to decide how strong you'd like your happy-hour cocktail. Wanna dump out half the ice through the planks at your feet, fill the glass with rum, and then splash a little cola on the bar? Not a problem. In fact, I was encouraged to do just that.

Cara instructed me to "continue [pouring the booze into your

HAPPY MATH The happy-hour special at the Dinghy was two euros per cocktail, a deal that could also be yours for two U.S. dollars. The glass I poured for myself had three generous ounces of Mount Gay rum with a splash of "cola." In comparison, that same beverage, with three shots of rum, in New York or L.A. would run you about eighteen dollars. Now that's happy math. Many guys I know would have no problem effectively earning back the five-hundred-dollar plane ticket during a week's vacation.

glass] until you feel like you might be sick the next morning," and I was happy to oblige.

The other interesting deal and questionable business practice is in their currency conversion—or the lack thereof. They treat euros and U.S. dollars one-to-one, which can work in your favor. The value of the dollar to the euro fluctuates on a daily basis. At the time I write this, the euro is stronger, so it would make sense to buy your drinks with dollars. If that changes, of course, you'll want to use euros (fingers crossed!).

French St. Martin

You'll know you're on the French side of the island when everything around you is suddenly in French. That's about the only noticeable difference. One of my favorite places on French St. Martin is actually just off of it. A five-minute ferry ride from the small town of Cul de Sac, at the north end of St. Martin, is Isle Pinel (Pinel Island). Make it

HOW TO MAKE TI PUNCH

This is not your typical sipping punch made with a load of delicious fruit flavors.

1 ounce white (un-aged) rum

½ ounce lime juice

½ ounce simple syrup (recipe below)

Serve in a wee glass with a small glass of water as a chaser.

French-speaking islands around the Caribbean include Martinique, Guadeloupe, Haiti, French Guiana, St. Barthélemy, and "portions" of St. Martin (the French side, duh!), Dominica, and St. Lucia.

HOW TO MAKE SIMPLE SYRUP

Simple syrup is a common sweetener found in most places that serve iced coffee or tea. The flavorings that you may add to your java at your favorite coffee establishment are basically simple syrup with added flavoring.

Stir sugar into an equal amount of water that's just been taken off of a boil.

Once the solution is cooled and capped, it will stay in liquid form.

part of your itinerary and it will likely be the most relaxing and gastronomically satisfying day of your trip. The last ferry off the island is at 4 P.M., so it's best to arrive in the morning. When you get there, you'll find topless French women, a quaint beach, and the Karibuni restaurant (voted one of the top ten restaurants in the Caribbean by *Condé Nast Traveler* in 2007).

Karibuni is a Swahili word meaning "welcome." Restaurant owner Eric Clement opened his first restaurant in Ghana but relo-

HOW TO MAKE A FRENCH MOJITO

The word mojito, *for one of Cuba's oldest cocktails, comes from the African word* mojo.

Mix mint, one teaspoon sugar, and lime juice in a glass. Muddle.

Add one ounce of rum.

Fill the glass with ice.

Top off with champagne.

cated to St. Martin in 1992. He was gracious enough to take me through the paces of local French St. Martin drinking, and I was gracious enough to let him.

He started us off with *ti* punch, which he said was a typical way to start the day on any of the French-speaking islands in the Caribbean. The world *ti* has nothing to do with tea, the drink, or the ti tree, a tropical plant. It's simply a shorter version of the word *petit,* meaning "small." So a ti punch is just a small punch. It's consumed with or without ice, as a shot, with the optional water chaser. Either way you have it, it's a small drink that really packs a punch.

French *mojitos,* just another example of the French wanting to claim everything delicious as their own, are also a Karibuni favorite. The drink is simply a mojito with the soda water replaced by champagne. Still, it was tasty, so instead of complaining, I ordered another.

Karibuni offers up one of the best spreads of seafood around. And by "around," I mean around the world. A typical meal could have fresh lobster (from cages just offshore), shrimp from Madagascar, freshwater river shrimp, smoked triggerfish, and conch fritters. It's the perfect marriage of French food, island drinks, and Caribbean living.

Dessert, in typical French fashion, contained alcohol. But it wasn't something you'd typically find in France. Tutu punch is made by tossing fresh mango, kiwi, pineapple, banana, dark rum, gold rum, and ice into a blender, and topping it off with a dash of cinnamon. I'd give you the recipe but—I just did. It's basically just a fruit smoothie blended with rum. If you can figure out how to make this punch taste bad, please never volunteer to mix me a drink.

Rum on a Hot Tin Roof

One hidden gem on French St. Martin is the Calmos Café. Along with serving up incredible fresh Caribbean fish dishes with a French twist, they also have a large selection of rooftop rums.

Their imported rums are infused with various fruits and spices with generous amounts of sugar in giant pickle jars. Then, in order to accelerate the infusion process, they place the jars on their corrugated, hot, tin roof for about a month. When the concoctions are fully "cooked," they strain them into repurposed bottles and cap them.

They offer rum infused with ginger, banana/vanilla, spices (which tastes like Captain Morgan Spiced Rum), coconut (which tastes like Malibu), mango, pineapple, and seemingly anything else they find lying around. Most (except one) of their concoctions are quite palatable, and go down easy—maybe too easy. Mary Poppins encouraged a spoonful of sugar to help the medicine go down; rooftop rum operates under a similar principle, times 100.

I can understand why one would add sugar to help the taste of a beverage; what I'm not quite sure about is why bugs are ever considered an improvement. I like alcohol and I like bugs, just not in the same place.

At the Calmos Café, Alex, the owner's son, looks over their most prized possession: a bottle of rum with several dead poisonous centipedes in it. To add insult to their death, the centipedes were put into the bottle alive. Then, when the overproof rum was poured into the bottle, they got very angry (understandably!) and took out their frustration on one another. The centipedes released their venom and bit each other, which made them literally shit with excitement. So what you're left with is a bottle of rum, five dead centipedes, their venom, and the last thing they used as a toilet.

Alex assured me that thanks to the sterilizing effect of rum, it's a concoction that's safe to drink. Why anyone would want to drink it is beyond me, but when has reason really stopped anyone from having a cocktail? ("Anyone," in this case, being me.) Incidentally, it tasted like all of its ingredients. I didn't enjoy the shot as much as I enjoyed being done with it. But I lived to talk about it, and sometimes that's enough.

Love Potion Number 9

If you have any friends who have visited St. Maarten, you will likely find a mini-bottle of guavaberry liqueur somewhere in their liquor cabinet. The Guavaberry Store is only a twenty-minute drive from the airport, so if you still have energy after your drinking tour of the island, stop by on the way home. The shop is quaint but touristy. The women dress in traditional Caribbean garb and offer tastings of a wide array of guavaberry products. Their flagship product is 70-proof guavaberry liqueur, which is really just imported rum infused with guavaberries and sugar. For aspiring horticulturists, guavaberries, also called rumberries, have nothing to do with guavas, and grow wild on the island. You can drink the liqueur straight (which I'd give a B-), mixed with champagne (B), or in a piña colada (an A, if you have an overdeveloped sweet tooth).

Before the owner, who is actually Irish, started mass-producing guavaberry rum, it had been made privately by locals for centuries. According to the Guavaberry Emporium, it still is the "national drink" of St. Maarten. And while guavaberries can be found on many Caribbean islands, as well as Hawaii and the Philippines, St. Martin has the highest concentration of the fruit. They do well in the island's dry climate and consistent warm temperatures (which hovers around 80 degrees year round). Until the mid-1900s, the liqueur was considered a Christmas drink, but it's now consumed year-round, mostly by tourists.

Along with guavaberry liqueur, the Emporium makes liqueurs with passion fruit, lime, spice, mango, almond, and a dozen others. You can also get "Love Potion Number 9," which they call "liquid Viagra." It's rum infused with *bois bande,* which literally translates into "erection wood." Erection wood trees grow abundantly in St. Maarten, and they are said to help obtain and maintain an erection. Okayyy . . . moving on.

Coconut Mon in da Mornin'

On a visit to the island, you will most likely wake at least once with a looming hangover. To cure your hangover in St. Maarten, you'll want to go to St. Martin, where they claim the best hangover remedy on the island. Marigot, the capital of French St. Martin, sits beneath an old French military outpost called Fort St. Louis, which was built from plans sent over by Louis XVI in 1767. In its shadow, on Wednesdays and Saturdays, is Marigot's sleepy open-air market, where you can find everything from locally grown fruits, vegetables, and spices to fresh fish, wooden art, and trinkets that you'll be excited about buying but will inevitably sell at your garage sale next year.

When you get to the market, look for the Coconut Juice House. They're known for serving up freshly squeezed juices, spiked with your favorite liquor. But the pièce de résistance is the fresh coconut, which the Coconut Juice House's Coconut Man insisted on spiking with gin. I've had fresh coconuts filled with a shot of rum and stabbed with a straw, but I'd never tried a coconut water spiked with anything else. Gin seemed a bit out of place. It's not tropical, like rum, nor is it even French. But I assumed that they knew something that I didn't, so I took a sip. Good. That is, "good to know that gin and coconut water taste horrible when mixed together." Trying to be polite, I said that was "not bad." So they mixed up another concoction: freshly pressed sugarcane juice, also mixed with gin. Also "not bad," which is another way of saying "not good."

As a hangover remedy, it's not far off the mark. It did have a little "hair of the dog." And while I hadn't consumed any gin on the island, it was reasonable to assume that a little booze might lift me out of my funk. The coconut water itself is, at least on paper, an excellent hangover remedy. In fact, the water inside a coconut has similar levels of sodium, potassium, and magnesium to those found in the human bloodstream. The water (without the gin) is very good at fighting dehydration, so much so that it has reportedly been used for intravenous rehydration of human subjects in emergency situations.

Remedy rating: *Inconclusive. If I hadn't been so turned off by the taste, it might actually have cured my hangover. But we'll never know . . .*

Chapter 10

Las Vegas

Latitude: 36°05' N

Longitude: 115°10' W

What they call it: Vegas, Sin City

What they speak: English

How to say cheers: I gotta hit the ATM again...

Hangover remedy: A hamburger

Las Vegas (lahs-VAY-gus) 1. The city that never sleeps. 2. Disney World for grown-ups. 3. A place where supposedly "what happens there, stays there" or, more accurately, "what you bring there [money] stays there."

Las Vegas, more affectionately known as just Vegas, is a place where photographs of our vacations tell more of the story than our "actual" memories of it. When you mix gambling, free booze, flashing lights, all-you-can-eat buffets, bachelor and bachelorette parties, strip clubs, labyrinthine casinos, and no clocks in a city that never sleeps, you know there's going to be trouble. But what happens in Vegas stays in Vegas. So, unless you have a tendency to walk around new cities with a video crew (and what kind of idiot would do that?), your secrets will be safe in the Entertainment Capital of the World.

Las Vegas literally means "the meadows," which is a surprisingly benign name for a city that's pretty much the American Sodom and Gomorrah. The Strip, which is what most people mean when they talk about Vegas (as opposed to the officially designated City of Las Vegas, which includes the flashing lights of the Strip but also a lot of quiet homes where regular people live regular lives), is just under four miles long. But the array of over-the-top hotels that glitter along those four miles contains enough decadence and drunkenness to bring a grown man to his knees, or at least leave him with a black eye . . . I know, because I was that man.

Sin City may seem like an odd place to feature in a drinking trav-

The Strip is 3.8 miles (6.1 kilometers) long. It's bordered at the southernmost point by Russell Road and to the north by Sahara Avenue.

elogue. It's not really known for producing any spirits. Nothing's really made in Las Vegas.

Free Drinks, at a Price

Most casinos offer free drinks to anyone gambling on their floor. Whether you're playing the nickel slots or throwing down thousand-dollar chips at the high rollers' table, the casino would love for you to "enjoy yourself" with a string of complimentary libations. But, as the odds are always in the house's favor, your free drink can end up costing you hundreds of dollars, or more, as you gamble away your children's college fund. Who knows, maybe little Bobby and Suzy will get scholarships! Screw it! Go all in! Split those tens! It'll teach them a good life lesson if they have to pay for college themselves.

The theory, as dependable as Einstein's Relativity, is that the more you drink, the more reckless your gambling will become. Patience, keen powers of observation, and luck are what you need to beat the house more consistently. Drinking drowns any possible advantage you might have.

Vegas is a place made for grown-ups. Sure, there may be things like a shark aquarium, the *Star Trek* experience (relocated from the Hilton to a mall), wave pools, and several roller coasters that make it seem like it's an appropriate place to bring the family. But that's only so the casinos can get a shot at Mommy and Daddy's money. The fact is that you must be twenty-one to gamble in Vegas. Many casinos will let you enter if you are eighteen, or younger if you're accompanied by an adult, but you may not gamble, stop at a table, or even hover nearby. The Bellagio currently has the strictest policy. You can't even enter the *hotel* if you aren't eighteen, unless you are a registered guest. Not even babies in strollers are allowed. But it's common knowledge that babies are extremely lucky, and drink copiously, so that makes sense. While you may be old enough to lay your life on the line for our country, and enter a casino, you need a few more years of maturing until you are ready to gamble and have a beer. Leave your fatigues and artillery at home.

Most of the cocktail waitresses' income comes from tips, so don't be a cheapskate. Of all the people working in that casino, she wants you to win more

The first drink book ever published in the United States was *The Bar-Tenders Guide, or The Bon-Vivant's Companion*. It was written in 1862 by "Professor" Jerry Thomas, an American bartender who popularized the art of the cocktail and is considered one of the first flair bartenders. At the height of his career, while working at the Occidental Hotel in San Francisco, he was earning $100 a week—more than the vice president.

than any of them. You win, she wins. The trick, as per a cocktail waitress whose ear I bent, is to tip big in the beginning. Once you've made a friend (and shown your friends what a generous person you are, even though they know that you're a penny-pinching scrooge back home), you can tip more modestly after the initial $10–$20 tip, because she knows that the more drunk you get, the more apt you are to once again loosen your grasp on your money.

Know When to Duck

In Vegas, they do everything just a little bit fancier than you would at home, and that is never more evident than at the Rio Las Vegas hotel and casino. The main floor of the casino looks like what Carnival in Rio would look like if it were organized by Disney executives on LSD. It's a bit tamer at the Voodoo Lounge, on the fifty-first floor of the hotel, until you order a drink. The bar is known for its cocktails, but better known for the manner in which they are mixed. They've got what those in the biz call "flair," not like what you'd use to signal a plane if you're stranded on an island—but possibly just as dangerous. Flair bartending is like a mix between a drink and a show, with bartenders who can juggle, throw, and flip bottles as well as pour them.

I spent some time with Tom, a competitive flair bartender who's proved that he is one of the best in the business. He's won some competitions, and after watching his dizzying routine, I could tell that he's worked extremely hard to hone his skills. But, since he's human, there's always room for error. Of course, nobody's perfect.

As I watched Tom flip, spin, and pour, he gradually made the house's signature cocktail, the Witch Doctor. Waiting for my drink, I wondered how long it would have taken him if I'd ordered two . . . By the time he was done, the glass, which was as big as a fishbowl, contained *nine* shots. And it was smoking like a proper witch's cauldron, a special effect caused by a dry-ice cube buried at the bottom of all of the regular ice. He stuck in about six straws (I was relieved that he didn't expect me to drink this on my own) and I took a sip. Because of all the sugar, the alcohol was nearly undetectable.

I was all set to close the scene when Curtiss Marlowe, the *Three Sheets* cameraman, asked if we could get one more shot of Tom doing his routine so the editors would have something to cut the scene up with. As I watched Tom, just off camera, I soon realized that, just like when you hop in the car and basically trust all of the other drivers on the road, I was giving Tom a little too much credit. In the middle of his routine, he lost the grip of a bottle and it flew through the air until it

HOW TO MAKE A WITCH DOCTOR SANS JUGGLING

Fill a fishbowl with dry ice and cover with regular ice.

Then add generous amounts of:

Pineapple rum

Coconut rum

Peach schnapps

White rum

Spiced rum

Grenadine

Pineapple juice

Sour mix

Dry ice is frozen CO_2. It's heavier than regular ice, so it sinks to the bottom of your drink, which is a very good thing, because it can cause frostbite. So you do *not* want to consume it. But as long as it's at the bottom, it makes a sweet drink look kind of spooky. That's because the sublimation of the frozen carbon dioxide causes it to go from a solid to a gas in one step, without pausing to become a liquid.

was stopped—by my face. Which quickly puffed up and left me with a black eye. Everyone felt bad for me, whereas I just felt bad for Tom. He was genuinely sorry, but I thought it made for killer television. And I kinda looked like a badass.

A Meeting with Mojo

The Bellagio hotel and casino has more master sommeliers than any one piece of property on the planet. In fact, since 1969 only 171 people have ever reached the status of being designated a master sommelier. More people have passed the test at NASA and actually gone into space than have passed the final exam at the Court of Master Sommeliers. Maybe that's because the astronauts don't have to go into the final exam hungover from studying all night! But what's even more astonishing than the fact that there are so few graduates is to know what it actually means to achieve the title of master sommelier. Along with hav-

ing to know generally everything there is to know about not only wine but beer, cigars (especially Cuban), and spirits, they must pass a final exam that reveals why only 171 people have completed the course. To complete their final test, the hopefuls are given four glasses of wine, two white and two red. They must, within twenty-five minutes, from tasting, smelling, and observing the qualities of the wine, be able to say what grape(s) were used in the wine, what country the wine came from, what wine region within that country it was produced in, and the kind(s) of grapes picked. Allow me to clar-ify, so you are appropriately impressed: They can drink, smell, and look at a glass of wine and tell the grape, country, region, and vintage. Not for one glass (which you might be able to guess with a little Vegas luck on your side), but four.

Tower

The Bellagio has a wine cellar five thousand bottles deep, and they have several restaurants (as well as room service) where you can tap into their stash. But for a more unique wine experience you might want to check out the Aureole, a Michelin-rated restaurant at the Mandalay Bay casino. In the middle of the restaurant stands a forty-two-foot, four-story tower made of steel and plexiglass that houses their wines. The *Mission: Impossible*–inspired wine "cellar" keeps 9,865 bottles stored at a comfortable 55 degrees and 70 percent hu-midity. It's not only an impressive sight, but offers a very respectable list of some of the world's finest wines.

Shaken, Not Stirred ... with Bacon

One of the strangest cocktails served in Sin City originated outside of the casinos, at the Double Down Saloon. They bill themselves as "the

Happiest Place on Earth" yet have a morbid logo of a skeleton with twigs growing out if its head. The bar is adorned with a "chaotic and psychedelic mural that covers every inch of walls and ceiling" while "disturbing videos come at you from all directions." Their signature cocktail fits in like a demon on a velvet poster under a black light: the bacon martini. The bottle sits at the bar, with several (formerly crispy) strips of bacon infusing themselves into the vodka.

HOW TO MAKE A BACON MARTINI

Cut five strips of bacon in half, lengthwise.

Bake the strips of bacon in the oven until crispy.

Put two strips aside, so you're left with eight.

Open a bottle of vodka and pour yourself a shot, to make room for the bacon.

Drop in the bacon (since they're thin, they'll fit into the bottle), put the cap back on the bottle, and let it sit for a few days. If you refrigerate, the fat will congeal, making it easier to scoop out.

Once your concoction is completed, pour two ounces into a shaker with ice, adding a half shot of dry vermouth. Shake, strain, serve.

Use the bacon strips that you put aside as swizzle sticks.

Get Fresh

Almost every bar, restaurant, hotel, and casino in Vegas has a hook. They have to have gimmicks to compete with the vast number of options. At Blush, an upscale nightclub located at the Wynn, they serve up "fresh" shots. Instead of using natural or bottled and pasteurized juices, they use fresh juices that they press on site to mix with their booze. But it's not just the typical juices like orange and lime. Their fresh shots are a combination of vodka (or tequila) and fresh juices, such as pineapple and strawberry, raspberry, and cantaloupe mixed with honeydew and watermelon. The fruits are muddled and passed through a strainer, leaving behind clear juices that are mixed with vodka or tequila.

From the Wynn to a Winning

In beer pong (also called "Beirut"), which is popular in colleges across the country, teams compete as they attempt to throw a Ping-Pong ball into their opponents' cups, which are lined up in a bowling-pin pattern across the table. The losers have to drink whenever a ball lands in their cup. It clearly illustrates the irony of drinking games, where the losers must drink, something they came there to do anyway.

But in Vegas, as the city does so well, the game is cranked up on steroids. Every year, Las Vegas hosts the "World Series of Beer Pong,"

BEER PONG

Top View

where upwards of one thousand mostly college-aged competitors vie for the grand prize. Players can either buy their way into the three-day tournament, as is done in Texas Hold 'Em tourneys, or win one of the satellite mini-tournaments held around the country. At the end, only one team will be victorious, and take home the fifty-thousand-dollar purse (a purse I wouldn't mind accessorizing with). Hand-to-eye-to-beer coordination and a tolerance for alcohol has its rewards.

Aces & Ales

Residents of Las Vegas don't have to go to the casinos to have a pint with friends. There is a bevy of local establishments that bring in the Las Vegans without the glitz and glamour of the tourist factories. Co-owned by Keri Kelli, lead guitarist for Alice Cooper, Aces & Ales is a down-home bar that serves up an excellent, constantly rotating selection of microbrews. Despite the fact that he has two girl names, Keri rocks hard and knows good beer. The sign outside—"Proudly leading the craft beer revolution. Love Beer, Love Life"—translates into a low-frills bar where locals, or tourists looking for a break, can shoot some pool, watch the game, and throw back a fairly formidable selection of lagers. Last time I was there I tried the Arrogant Bastard, Rogue Hazelnut, Moylan's Kilt Lifter Scotch Ale, Unibroue La Fin du Monde, Weihenstephaner Hefe, and Dogfish Head 90 Minute IPA. Let's just say my arrival is a much clearer memory than my departure...

Feed Your Face and Starve Your Wallet

Many of the more popular hangover remedies entail filling your belly to replace your headache with the sensation of having eaten too much. Blood rushes to your stomach, leaving your brain in a food coma. On the Vegas Strip, in typical style, they do things their own way. Why pay $10 for a burger when you can pay $777? Sure, you could buy a pretty nice mountain bike to ride to work occasionally or tool around with on the weekends while you got in shape. You could buy Mom a new washer and dryer. Or you could buy a Big Mac (just under $4) once a week for the next four years . . . But chances are, if you can afford the triple-seven burger, then you already have a trainer, your Mom has someone do her laundry for her, and you haven't eaten at Mickey D's in a decade. So, enjoy.

This burger, at the Paris Hotel & Casino, is amazing. But not $777 amazing. The fact that it comes with a bottle of Dom Pérignon Rosé and is served by a butler (if you're staying in the hotel) starts to make it more reasonable. If you want it the way I had it, it'll cost you closer to $20,777. Just reserve the Napoleon suite, which goes for a reasonable $20,000 per night. Or, if times are tight, pull up your bootstraps and go downstairs to Le Burger Brasserie and do without the champagne. There you can grab the same burger for $65. Almost sounds reasonable at this point, doesn't it?

HOW TO ASSEMBLE YOUR OWN $65 BURGER

1 all-Kobe-beef patty

Caramelized onions

Sliced prosciutto

Sliced Brie cheese

Australian freshwater lobster

Hundred-year-old balsamic vinegar

Remedy rating: *Three out of Three Sheets. Sitting in bed while eating a massive burger might put it at the top on its own. But adding a little hair of the dog (not that I specifically had champagne the night before) solidifies it as one of the top three hangover remedies I've ever ingested.*

Asia and Oceania

Nestled between the Indian Ocean and the Pacific Ocean, the neighboring continents of Asia and Oceania offer vastly diverse traveling experiences. Some are fascinating, some are incredible, some are terrifying, and some are just downright nauseating. Leaving the temples for the tour buses, this section will get close up with the alleys, markets, bars, restaurants, vineyards, and backyards where you can have a seat, take a sip, and let it all sink in. In Taipei, Taiwan, you can eat crickets instead of french fries, get a foot massage that will leave you limping but happy, and never, ever have an empty glass. In Queenstown, New Zealand, you can drink fine wines, let someone strap you to a harness and push you off a bridge, and then have your host light a bar on fire. And in Japan you'll drink sake, lots of it.

Chapter 11

Taipei

Latitude: 25°02' N

Longitude: 121°31' E

What they call it: China

What they speak: Mandarin, Taiwanese

How to say cheers: *Gan bei!* (Cheers!) for traditionalists; *Otada* (Let it dry!) for the modernists

Hangover remedy: Painful foot massage

MAINLAND CHINA

Taipei

TAIWAN

Taipei (tie-PAY) 1. The capital of Taiwan, an island located one hundred miles off the coast of mainland China. 2. The birthplace of many of your major appliances. 3. A city where the beer is made from rice, the booze is made from grass, and cocktails can be made from snakes.

Some travel experiences create lasting impressions, while others are more like permanent emotional scars. In Taipei, you can get both. From meaningful customs and gestures of goodwill to snake genitals, fried bugs, and foot pummeling, Taipei will cross things off your bucket list that weren't there in the first place.

Taipei is the capital of Taiwan, an island about the size of Maryland that sits off the coast of mainland China. Finding the country on a map is simple, but understanding the politics is a bit more confusing. Taiwanese people call their country "China," but so do the people living in that communist monolith to the west. The official name of Taiwan is "the Republic of China," which was established as a democratic nation just after World War II. Originally, the ROC label covered not only Taiwan, but also all of mainland China. That all changed during the communist revolution, when the mainland was declared the "the *People's* Republic of China." A lot has happened since then, and if this were a geopolitical textbook, I might go into more detail. But it's not. So let's hit the bar!

When drinking in Taiwan, the traditional toast is "Gan bei!" (often mispronounced as "Gam pei"), which is similar to "Kanpai!" (often mispronounced "Kampai") in Japan, and both generally mean "Cheers!" The more modern toast is "Otada!" which means "Let it dry." And you often hear even non-English-speaking Taiwanese calling out "Let it dry" in English.

Fishing for Fun

Most people know little more about Taiwan than the fact that their TV was made there. And while that may very well be the case, Taipei is an important and bustling metropolis that at times looks like New York City and at others resembles ancient Asia. Centuries-old temples are bookended by electronics stores and dim sum houses. And the busy streets are clogged with a sea of motor scooters, small cars, and bicycles traveling in unison like a colossal flock of pigeons. Yet somehow, in the midst of all the chaos, the people of Taipei are generally warm and welcoming.

In an area of Taipei called the Seafood Restaurants, in the Ling Seng North Road neighborhood, you'll not only find lots of fish, but also many suitable groups who will be pleased to indulge your anthropological expedition into Taiwanese drinking. I hooked up with my group at Central Market Fresh Seafood in the Seafood Restaurants district.

Back in the day, this area of the city was traditionally where locals bought their fish to prepare for their family meals. But over time, street vendors moved in and began cooking the fish and serving it as snacks, and eventually restaurants and bars popped up as well. Eating and drinking in Taipei, especially when the sun goes down, go hand in hand. Rarely is one done without the other. So when the lights come on, it's less about getting fish on ice and more about getting ice-cold drinks.

Taiwan Beer

If you're drinking beer in Taiwan, there's a more than 80 percent chance that you're drinking the national brand, aptly named Taiwan Beer. Not even Guinness in Ireland (since the 1970s) or Bud in the States has had that high a market share.

Outside of Taiwan, however, it's much more difficult to find. Despite attempts at export, Taiwan Beer remains relatively unknown off the island. You may find it stateside in Taiwanese communities, but you're going to still have to search for it. And please don't go asking for it in Thai restaurants, like Steve McKenna did; that's Thai-*land* not Tai-*wan*. Your best chance of finding it is in a Chinese restaurant, but more often than not, Tsingtao, from mainland China, will be the beer they've imported to accompany your General Tso's chicken and side of broccoli.

Taiwan Beer has been around since 1919. Back then, Taiwan was a Japanese colony. The governor's office borrowed some beer-making equipment from Hawaii, and some beer-brewing strategies from the Germans, and Taiwan Beer was born.

Taiwan Beer is a slightly sweet, light lager that goes down easy, especially when it's chilled. It doesn't have much body or a hoppy flavor like some more complex-tasting beers, and is really more for wetting your whistle than it is for savoring. Though Taiwan Beer looks like beer, smells like beer, and tastes like beer, in Germany it wouldn't be considered beer and couldn't be labeled as such. According to the Reinheitsgebot, the German purity law of 1516, to call a product "beer" it must be made of barley, yeast, water, and hops—nothing more. While Taiwan Beer is made with the traditional beer ingredients, it's also brewed with rice.

In 2004, the People's Republic of China refused to allow importation of Taiwan Beer to mainland China. They cited a law that states that regional names cannot be used on commercial products. The Taiwanese point out that it's a bit hypocritical, because the Chinese-made Tsingtao beer is named after the coastal city of Qingdao. Silly communists…

The brewery that produces Taiwan Beer was built in 1919, during the Japanese colonial era, and was the only brewery on the island at the time. After Taiwan's retrocession (when it once again became China) in 1945, the plant was placed under the authority of the Taiwan Provincial Tobacco and Liquor Monopoly Board. Its name was subsequently changed to the Taipei Beer Company and, later, to the Taipei Second Brewery. In 1975, it was officially named the Chienkuo Brewery, which it is called to this day.

As weird as beer made with rice may seem, it's a lot more common than you think. The "King of Beers," Budweiser, is also made with rice. The rice reduces bitterness, ups the sweetness a bit—and it's cheap, which helps corporate giants generate more beer for your buck. Just like Bud, Taiwan Beer isn't a very flavorful brew. And just like a Bud, an ice-cold Taiwan Beer on a warm and humid evening totally hits the spot.

Date

Taipei 101 is one of the world's tallest buildings. Although it's designed to look like a bamboo stalk, it more closely resembles a stack of Chinese takeout boxes—especially if you're hungry, or drunk, or both. At 1,600 feet tall, it's a whopping 400 feet taller than the Empire State Building. And since the average height of the buildings surrounding it is about five floors, Taipei 101 sticks out like seven-foot-six NBA star center Yao Ming in, well, Taipei. Built to be the world's tallest building in 2004, it's already been passed by Burj Dubai, which has it by 250 feet. But one record it still holds (at least at time of printing) is for having the fastest elevator. You can go from the ground floor to the 101st in thirty-seven seconds. That's faster than the elevator in my Taipei hotel got me from the lobby to the sixth floor— no kidding, I timed it.

Wait...Didn't I Just Drink My Beer?

In college, my buddy Steve McKenna and I tried to join the "century club" with the goal of drinking a shot of beer (one ounce) every minute for 100 minutes. At first it seemed easy, even boring, but after twenty minutes, I realized that it would leave me incredibly intoxicated (it's more than eight bottles in an hour and a half). I quit. Steve finished.

Drinking Taiwan Beer reminded me a little bit of this game. Oftentimes you're not sipping it, but in fact throwing back the entire glass in one shot. Thankfully the glasses are only about six ounces, and only get filled up with about four to five ounces of beer, but sometimes the seemingly meager size can work against you. It's easy to assume that you're not drinking that much, which means you may lose track of how many you've put away.

Taiwanese social etiquette dictates that it's not *your* duty to make sure your glass is full, it's *everyone else's*—just as it's *your* duty to make sure *everyone else* has a full beer. When you see an empty beer, you attack it. You don't bother asking the person if they'd like another. Individual desire is irrelevant. Besides, if you did ask them, they'd have to say yes. In Taiwan, most people want to save face by not saying no. In fact, there isn't even a specific word for no in Chinese, as there is in the English language. "No" is achieved by restating the negative of the question. If someone asked you if you wanted more beer, your response would be "not more." But even if you did say "not more," the response would be a laugh, a joke, and another full beer.

Be forewarned: As a newcomer, it's difficult to fly under the radar and drink less than the group. In a culture where they take very good care of their guests, you'll find yourself drinking more than anyone else at the table.

Indian Beer House

No trip to Taipei is complete without a stop at a beer house, of which the city has an abundance. Many of them serve other drinks as well, but their main purpose is beer, beer, and most of all, beer. Oh, and crickets. Oh, and beer.

If you want to look like you're in the know, head to the popular Indian Beer House. How it got its name is a mystery to me. There's nothing even remotely Indian about the place. Unless you count dinosaur bones as Indian, which I don't. Because everything is done up in a dino motif, from the floors to the ceilings, to the T-rex skull urinals (yes, you read that correctly). And when you sit down, the waitress brings you a mini-barrel of beer, which holds about a gallon of brew. And, as I found, just like with glasses of beer, barrels don't sit empty for very long in a beer house.

One of the most popular food items on the menu is fried crickets. They come in a big bowl, like french fries. In fact, each cricket comes with a french fry shoved up its ass (what a way to go). It's uncomfortable to look at at first, but after a few beers and one bite, you'll be chomping on them like supersized, super-crispy fries—with eyes. Truth be told, the french fry is the major flavor component, with the insect adding an extra crunch. No ketchup, no sauce, just add a dash of salt and pop that bad boy in your mouth.

Holy Kaoliang, Batman

Kaoliang (gáo-lee-ong), the most popular Taiwan-made booze, comes from fermented sorghum, which is in the grass family and is similar to sugarcane. Kinmen, one of the most popular brands of kaoliang, is made on the island of Kinmen, which is to the west of Taiwan, close to mainland China. The kaoliang that you'll find in Taipei can be as strong as 58 percent alcohol. That's 116 proof. Meaning that drinking one ounce of kaoliang would be the equivalent of downing one and a half ounces of tequila.

If your experience in Taipei is anything like mine, you may find yourself ordering a bottle of kaoliang for a table of locals and getting a reaction you might not expect. In my case, the group suddenly fell quiet, as if just the sight of the bottle triggered anxiety. As locals, I realized, they had all had a past with kaoliang, like most Americans have with tequila. I could see flashbacks flicker across their faces—the night they went streaking, threw up in the back of a friend's car, or woke up in a strange place, quietly collected their clothes, and bolted. They all knew firsthand where our night would be headed if we cracked open the kaoliang. Me? I was about to find out. Because, as I turned to take in the group to my left, there he was: Steve McKenna.

Sorghum was introduced to the United States in the 1800s and is found mostly in the plains states and some parts of the South. We use it to make sugary sorghum syrup. Unfortunately (or fortunately), we haven't expanded our use of sorghum to include alcoholic beverages.

It wasn't *the* Steve McKenna, but it was clearly his Taiwanese counterpart. He was tossing back the kaoliang like we were tossing back our beer. My table wouldn't touch the stuff, and this guy couldn't keep his hands off it. And it showed. I approached him and asked if I could sit with him and his friend for a moment. He gave me a toothy grin and started pouring. I now had a six-ounce glass filled with three ounces of kaoliang (the equivalent of nearly five shots of

Drinking, in my experience, makes people more prone to 39
lighting up. While smoking is quite popular in Taipei, they
have an alternative method of satisfying an oral fixation and
a craving for a nicotine-like buzz. *Bīnláng* (be-yin-lang), or
betel nut, is chewed to produce a sensation similar to tobacco and give you energy (as well as causing sweating and
hot flashes). The betel nuts are popular with partiers, as well
as taxi drivers and truck drivers looking for a little help stay-
ing awake. They are usually sold at roadside stands, wrapped
in a leaf (from the unrelated betel pepper plant) with lime
paste. The stands where they are sold, in an effort to compete with one another, have resorted to employing girls in
skimpy outfits (called betel nut girls) to peddle their nuts.
Actually, it's not a nut at all, but rather a seed from the betel
palm, and resembles a small, unripe acorn.

tequila). I poured half of it back into *his* glass, and we downed them.
Pow! Zap! It crossed my mind that this stuff would be handy for
starting a campfire but seemed barely suitable for consumption. It
wasn't tasty like whiskey or cognac; in fact it had no real taste at all,
other than of pure alcohol. It also tasted like trouble. So after tossing
back my shot, I left Taiwan Steve to go and find some.

Snake Alley

Unlike some destinations with misleading names, like Red Square in
Moscow, which is neither "red" nor "square," Snake Alley is exactly
what it claims to be: an alley with snakes. For foreigners, it's easier to
say "Snake Alley" than "Hwahsi Jie," and it's one of the few places in
the city where Westerners don't stick out like a sore thumb. But the
plethora of tourists doesn't detract from its authenticity. Although
it's not exceedingly popular with most of the city's residents, Snake

Alley is still a twenty-four-hour market that sells all sorts of traditional remedies to locals, with one ingredient being most popular: snakes. What's more, they have an alcoholic serpentine concoction that I couldn't leave Taipei without trying. No matter how much I may have wanted to.

Although it's one of the oldest markets in Taipei, Snake Alley is really just a single-aisled bazaar lined with trinket shops and exotic butchers. Don't be deterred by the fluorescent supermarket-type lighting—you won't be finding any of this stuff in your local grocery store. A few paces into the alley and you're surrounded by disemboweled snakes hanging from the rafters with their blood dripping into bowls. Yummy. (You can't help but be curious how many health violations would be issued if this place were in the States.) How has a location that has been in business since before the Pilgrims settled the New World survived this long if the food is so, in a word, disgusting? Still, I simply couldn't travel this far and not experience what the fuss was all about. How could anyone take a stroll down this corridor without partaking in the unique delicacies it has to offer? Very easily . . .

As I ambled down the alley like a prisoner on the green mile, I was only vaguely aware of what awaited me. A few hundred yards in, I found my calling—or, rather, it found me. An attractive and unusually tall Taiwanese woman sporting a headset microphone like a Time-Life operator was beckoning to the crowd gathering in front of her shop, with the flair of a sideshow barker. She was wielding several nonvenomous snakes, including an albino boa constrictor, and dangling a mouse (dinner) by its tail as she carried on in Chinese about something that seemed very important. After she'd slyly lured enough people in to see what the fuss was about, she introduced a tray with several shot glasses of earthy-colored liquids. I knew that it was now or never.

The tray of shots looked relatively innocuous, but their aromas were anything but. The combination of all the shots smelled like a dirty fish tank that's home to a content yet inactive turtle (long story, but just know that I'm right). My new pal sat down, handed me the first glass, and gestured at me to drink. All I could think to myself was *You don't know what that stuff is. You're in a foreign country. Make her drink it first.* Here I was at a sketchy night market in a distant land with someone I'd never met who was trying to feed me indiscernible shots. Who knows, she might have been about to feed me poison. In fact— she was.

My host agreed to drink first. As soon as she was done with hers, I reached for mine. It looked like a Bloody Mary, which wasn't far from the truth. That is, if the American version contained actual blood. The glass contained a mixture of cobra's blood, kaoliang, and a touch of honey. It tasted like a cross between blood, cheap rum, and what a decaying snake smells like.

Apparently, this first shot was an aphrodisiac. Truthfully, the only "desire" I felt was the strong urge to vomit. Knowing it would have tasted even worse on the way up, I did not.

I assumed the nastiest stuff was behind me. I was wrong. The next shot was called

Snakes, the lucky SOBs, have not just one penis, but two. When mating, the snakes get to choose which one to use. The penises themselves have barbs at the end, which makes escaping from intercourse impossible for the female until the barbs are no longer engorged. And unlike the "blink-and-you'll-miss-it" sex that humans have (or is it just me?), these phallic friends go at it for up to twenty hours. T-w-e-n-t-y hours. It's no wonder they think snake parts increase virility: two wieners and twenty hours of sex? Get that reptile some Gatorade and a cigarette!

"poison." It was a mixture of cobra's venom and kaoliang and looked like dirty lemonade. The benefit? It was supposed to be good for my skin. I'm waiting for any youthful effects to kick in. Still nothing...

Shot number three? Snake bile, once again mixed with kaoliang. Bile, of course, is an alkaline fluid secreted by the liver. This bile was vile. Why drink it? This wonderful potion is believed to be good for the eyes. I wore contacts when I walked in. And, yup, still wearing 'em. In fact, I believe my eyesight has since gotten worse.

The last shot looked like used cooking oil. And after drinking it, I wish it had been. It was kaoliang that had been sitting in a bottle with *snake penises* and *testicles*. Do I need to repeat myself for the proper effect? It was supposedly another aphrodisiac. And it was definitely repulsive.

A glutton for punishment, I asked to see the bottle that this last shot came from. The repurposed bottle, which was clearly originally produced by my good friend Jack Daniel, was now the proud vessel of kaoliang and about one hundred fully intact snake genitals. It looked like something from a science lab—an evil, demented science lab. The mad scientist reached into the bottle with her chopsticks, pulled out a frank-and-beans combo, and dropped them into a shot glass for me. Noooo thanks. I offered up $100, then $200, and finally $300 to any member of the crowd foolish enough to eat it. And like a cobra striking its prey, Eric-the-Sound-Guy (he prefers to be called a "sound engineer," but he's neither sound, nor a driver of trains, so I refuse to call him that) snatched the money and went for it. About five minutes later he got hot flashes and started sweating. Moments later he disappeared into a back room, and what happened afterward is still a mystery, because he refused to tell us.

Hangover Remedy: Pain

The ultimate hangover remedy in Taiwan, according to the locals, is a foot massage. Head to the Hsin Tien Gong Temple area and you'll find a cluster of foot massage clinics beckoning you with the promise of hangover relief, along with a laundry list of other ailments they can cure. But don't expect a calming, peaceful experience. I was, and I could not have been more wrong.

The diminutive Chinese man I visited managed to inflict pain on my feet the likes of which I'd never experienced. He beat the living shit out of my feet. He applied pressure with his thumbs and knuckles that was so painful I thought I'd pass out.

Why go through this torturous pain to relieve another kind of pain? My "masseuse" told me that certain points on the feet are directly connected to different parts of the body. The point he focused on was directly connected to my headache. Given the vigor with which he dug in, truth be told, I wondered if I had inadvertently insulted his mother.

After sixty minutes, you'll be done. At that point you'll find that any symptoms of being hungover have been replaced with throbbing feet.

All in all, Taipei was an amazing city. It's where the old meets the new, the traditional bumps up against the modern, and the young and the old manage to coexist. It's a city rich in customs and light in spirit. And it's a great place to drink snake penises, eat bugs, and get the crap beaten out of your soles. Your headache won't be any less painful, but the bruises on your feet will be a welcome distraction.

Remedy rating: *Two out of Three Sheets. I've often had hangovers improve in an hour period the next morning. I can go from "I want to go back to bed" at*

10 A.M. to "*I guess I could drink*" at 11 A.M. *So I can't say whether the treat-
ment actually helped. It really was as painful as I made it out to be, so my
hangover may have just gotten scared out of my body. I'm tempted to give it
a Three out of Three Sheets rating, but as the results are somewhat open to
interpretation, I'll stick with my Two out of Three rating.*

Chapter 12
New Zealand

Latitude: 41°17' S

Longitude: 174°27' E

What they call it: New Zealand, Aotearoa (Maori)

What they speak: English, Maori, New Zealand Sign Language

How to say cheers: Cheers! (English), *Kia ora!* (Maori)

Hangover remedy: Adrenaline and fear for your life

Auckland
NEW ZEALAND
North Island
South Island
Queenstown

New Zealand (nu-ZEE-lund) 1. An isolated island nation. 2. A country that offers unspoiled landscapes, vineyards, glaciers, and bungee jumping. 3. Where Hobbits live peacefully in the Shire, the elves live happily in Rivendell, and the ring of power was forged and destroyed (or more accurately, where *The Lord of the Rings* trilogy was filmed).

New Zealand lives by its lonesome in the South Pacific, about 1,250 miles southeast of Australia. The whole country is about the size of New York State and Pennsylvania combined, and its entire population is roughly 4.3 million, about half that of New York City.

New Zealanders, aka Kiwis, live on the country's North and South islands. Three quarters of the population lives on the smaller, warmer North Island, while the South Island is larger, with a more diverse and storied drinking culture. The two islands are separated by the Cook Strait. To get from one side to the other, it's easy to take a ferry. Or, you could swim—the distance is only fourteen miles at its narrowest point. Sure, there are sharks, and some of the meanest currents and most unpredictable weather on the planet. But you could do it. More than sixty people have already. Okay, fine, take a ferry. I really thought you were tougher than that. Me? Oh, no, I didn't swim it. Why? Uh . . . let's get back to the book.

New Zealand is so far from other places that one can only imagine how frustrating—and expensive, and time-consuming—it must be to import goods. So in New Zealand, not surprisingly, they're very DIY (do-it-yourself). They toast successful bungee jumps with a locally made premium vodka named for the 42nd parallel, which runs through Wellington, the southernmost city on the North Island. They make local beers on both islands. They are known for producing some award-winning world-class wines. And their whiskey used to be made at home, by Scottish immigrants who brought their love of Scotch and their knowledge of distillation techniques with them when they left the highlands and settled in the Hokonui Hills.

The Polynesians are suspected to be the first people to have arrived on the islands of New Zealand between seven hundred and two thousand years ago. They call themselves the Maori. In Maori, New Zealand is called Aotearoa, which means "The Land of the Long White Cloud." When the first Europeans arrived in 1642, the ones that weren't killed off by the Maori fled back home to the Netherlands. It wasn't until 1769 that Europeans, this time the Brits, returned to New Zealand, where they've been visiting ever since.

Whiskey in a Jar

To get my education on New Zealand whiskeys, I ventured to the South Island for a chat with Malcom Willmott, co-owner of Southern Distilleries, the world's southernmost distillery, based out of Timaru. We were joined by New Zealand whiskey historian Jim Geddes, who runs the Hokonui Moonshine Museum, located in the town of Gore (which also claims it invented the Internet). For an authentic experience, I met up with Malcom and Jim in an area significant to the roots of New Zealand whiskey—a sheep-shearing cabin in the Hokonui Hills, just outside Gore.

Before 1865, whiskey production in New Zealand was widespread. When the government realized that taxing alcohol could net them a hefty profit, they introduced the Distillation Act, which enforced a high tax on distilleries, thus prohibiting smaller outfits from being able to turn a profit. This shut down the smaller distillers and even made it difficult for the bigger companies to continue making the stuff. After the dust settled, only two producers remained: the New Zealand Distilling Company, out of Dunedin on the South Island, and Crown Distilleries, of Auckland on the North Island.

But the Kiwis, many of them immigrants from Scotland, were too fond of their whiskey to go without it. Their two options were expensive Scotches brought all the way from Scotland, or poor-quality whiskey from Australia. So some of the Scots took it upon themselves to start making their own. Illegally. Ooooo.

One of these entrepreneurial Scots was the widow Mary McRae, who boarded the ship *Hydaspes* in 1872 in Scotland, with seven children and a small copper still, and wound up in the Hokonui Hills.

She had eight mouths to feed, so she set up shop with her oldest son as the distiller. With her training back home

Mary McRae distributed her whiskey in whatever containers were available. She worked with what she had, which had the added benefit of making it more difficult for authorities to keep tabs on her product.

in the whisky industry, the new business was a quick success. The ingredients of sugar and yeast were easy to find, although malted barley was tougher to come by. But once she was in operation, she could easily exchange a bottle— or a jar or a milk jug—of her finished product, now called Hokonui, for a bushel of barley from the local farmers.

> The most important piece of the still was the copper condensing coil, also called the "worm." A still was not difficult to build, but without the worm it was worthless. When batches were being distilled in the woods, the still master would never leave the worm behind. But still masters would often share a worm with other still masters, especially if the other distillers had theirs confiscated and destroyed by the fuzz.

Ideally, Mary would have aged her whiskey in oak barrels for several years. But, due to the demand, there wasn't even time for it to be aged for a week. In order to elude the authorities, she added honey to make the coloring closer to what people would expect from commercial whiskey, and to make it not easily discernable from the expensive Scotch being imported from across the globe. And since her product tasted better than anything besides the overpriced Scotch, people didn't mind.

> In 1902, most Presbyterian Scots pushed for prohibition. And they got it. It wasn't a countrywide ban, but was put to a vote in each town. In the Hokonui area, this just pushed the production underground, forcing people to make it by the light of the moon, hence the term "moonshine."

Currently, Old Hokonui is produced by Southern Distilleries. Their label has the phrase "Passes all tests except the police" as well as a skull and crossbones and the Latin saying *Ergo bibamus,* which translates as "So, let us drink." Ah, marketing. Southern Distilleries also makes a product similar to Baileys Irish Cream. Both are liqueurs, made from whiskey and cream, but the Old Hokonui Whiskey Cream is sweetened with honey and mint. It's best served over ice, and quite delightful with a sprig of mint.

Unless you have a license to sell alcohol, in New Zealand any product distilled on your property cannot be sold, and must be consumed on your property.

Kiwi (the people, not the fruit) Wine

Wines have been made in New Zealand since the colonists arrived. But while the oldest vineyard was established by the Roman

Kia ora is Maori for "hello" or "good day," and according to the New Zealand Ministry for Culture and Heritage, it's one of a hundred Maori words every New Zealander should know.

Catholic Church in 1851, it is only in recent decades that New Zealand's wines have gotten high grades from wine snobs the world over. New Zealand gets attention these days for their wonderful sauvignon blanc, especially from the Marlborough region. With extra points for the rich-in-minerals soils and the climate, if you're an oenophile visiting New Zealand, you definitely want to spend some time tracking down the country's best vintages. (If you're not one,

A GUIDE TO NEW ZEALAND'S WINE COUNTRY

Northland	Cabernet sauvignon, merlot, chardonnay
Auckland	Cabernet sauvignon, merlot, chardonnay, pinot gris
Gisborne	Chardonnay
Hawkes Bay	Chardonnay, sauvignon blanc, viognier, cabernet sauvignon, merlot, cabernet franc, syrah, pinot noir
Wellington	Pinot noir, riesling, syrah, pinot gris, cabernet franc
Nelson	Chardonnay, sauvignon blanc, riesling, pinot noir
Marlborough	Sauvignon blanc, chardonnay, riesling, sparkling wines
Central Otago	Pinot noir, chardonnay, sauvignon blanc, riesling, pinot gris, gewürztraminer

SCREW IT If you buy a bottle of wine in New Zealand and bring it on a picnic, there's a good chance you won't need to pack a corkscrew. Ninety-five percent of the wines that are made in New Zealand for the domestic market come with screw caps.

you probably don't know what an oenophile is, but I'm sure you can figure it out.)

The North and South islands are home to a range of

With upwards of 100 million sheep in New Zealand, they outnumber people 22 to 1.

vineyards that produce a good deal of reds, whites, and even sparkling wines. The Otago Valley, the world's southernmost wine region, is a wonderful place to sample some excellent pinot noirs. Gisborne, the world's easternmost wine region (in relation to the International Date Line), has some top-notch chardonnays, sun-kissed each morning before the rest of the world is even awake.

For extra credit, visit Waiheke Island, near Auckland. The Stonyridge Vine-

What do Jamaica and New Zealand have in common? 1. They are both islands. 2. Both are great places to get your drink on. 3. When she visits, the queen of England is the Queen. She's either the queen of Jamaica or of New Zealand, although it is primarily a symbolic position, holding no real power. (The government is run by a democratically elected parliament.)

yard produces Larose, an organic bordeaux blend. This premium, estate-grown wine is prestigious, expensive, and loved worldwide by those in the know.

Hail to the Queenstown

While you can sip local wine almost anywhere in New Zealand, if you're looking for a little more excitement, by far the most extreme place to go is Queenstown. It's a small resort town of about twenty thousand people (not including the tourists) that sits at an inlet of Lake Wakatipu, a long, icy lake formed by glaciers. From Queenstown, you get a remarkable view of the Remarkables, an aptly named mountain range that rises above the town. At any time of year, you can sample a range of extreme sports in Queenstown, like bungee jumping, jet-boating, white-water rafting, and several other extreme activities popular during the summer, peaking in December. The winter frolicking, frivolity, and life-risking peaks in July.

> Rugby is the unofficial national sport of New Zealand, with the "All Blacks" being the favorite team. Before each game, the team performs the *haka*, a intimidating challenge dance of the Maori.

They say, although it would be a logistical implausibility, that Queenstown actually has more bars than it has people. I counted. There are more people—but not by a lot.

The Other Hillary

Sir Edmund Hillary is a hero in New Zealand. As the first man to have summited the 29,028-foot Mount Everest in 1953, he's a legend in his country. He was also knighted and can be viewed whenever one buys coffee or chocolates in New Zealand, as his face is displayed prominently on the New Zealand five-dollar bill.

He is also celebrated via a cocktail at a bar in Queenstown that should not be missed. Eichart's, located just off the lake, is a wonderful and surprisingly upscale hotel where I slept off my hangovers. They've got a bar that serves up a unique drink named for Sir Edmund Hillary, made with a local vodka called 42 Below. The drink was created for a national cocktail competition by Dan-the-Bartender.

Dan's inspiration to create the Sir Edmund? The ingredients that Sir Edmund would have had with him on his historic climb. Dan starts by muddling apricots, honey, and lemon juice in a glass. Then he adds two shots of 42 Below, which he has previously infused with dates for a few weeks. It's then topped off with Nepalese masala tea, and shaken with ice. The last addition is a Sir Edmund (the five-dollar bill) fashioned into a flag and taped to the end of a straw, which the customer may keep after being overcharged by about five dollars.

42 Below

42 Below is named for the 42nd parallel, but it also happens to be the alcohol percentage of the vodka (which is 84 proof). This is one marketing gimmick (at least, I'm assuming it wasn't an accident) that might raise the vodka's profile (it got me to mention it, didn't it?). But that also raises its duty when it's imported into the United States, since the duty is typically based on alcohol reduced to 80 proof.

42 Below offers a premium vodka, as well as several flavored vodkas, including *feijoa* (also known as pineapple guava), manuka honey (honey harvested from bees who have visited the flowering manuka shrub), passion fruit, and kiwi (I'm assuming it's infused with the fruit, not the bird . . . or the people).

According to the company, their vodka is superior because the resources in New Zealand are so unspoiled. The water used to make it comes from under an extinct volcano, where everyone knows the best water comes from . . . Oh, and here I thought I was getting great water from my fridge.

Barley wine is a specific style of beer that has an alcohol content of more than 8 percent. These beers have typically around the same alcohol percentage as wine, which is where they got their name. But they are true beers, not wines, as they contain no fruit.

World Bar

World Bar is a great place for a world traveler to get his drink on. You can toss your tip (coins) into a brass horn over the bar (trying not to break something in the process) and grab a bite or some drinks. They're best known for serving up teapots full of your favorite drinks, which you pour as shots. Each bottomless-seeming teapot will pour about fifteen shots, in flavors such as the Ginja Ninja (Canadian Club, Stones Ginger, melon, dry ginger ale), Horny Monkey (Kahlua, banana schnapps, Canterbury cream), Mud Wrestler (Southern Comfort, butterscotch, Amaretto, chocolate, milk), and, of course, everyone's favorite wrangler in Palm Springs, the Cocksucking Cowboy (butterscotch schnapps, Canterbury cream) . . .

They also offer a variety of ciders, including their "house ale," Loopy Juice. It's called Loopy Juice because its alcohol content is higher than most New Zealand beers. But 5 percent wouldn't be considered "loopy" in the United States. That's the same alcohol content of a Budweiser or Woodchuck Cider.

THE SIX O'CLOCK SWILL During World War I, the morality police established a new drinking order in New Zealand. Pubs and bars were only open after the end of the workday for one hour, and were closed on Sundays, so men who wanted to "relax" after a day at the office, in the mills, or in the fields would rush to drink as much as they could from first call to last call. Much to the pleasure of hardworking men across the country, this practice was discontinued by the end of the 1960s.

Hail to the Cook

The Cook Strait is named for James Cook, who in 1770 was the first European commander to sail between the islands. Cook did something else that was noteworthy—the English explorer was the first to have beer brewed in New Zealand. Cook's beer was made with wort, with the addition of molasses and rimu bark and leaves. The good captain believed that beer would cure scurvy, a disease common to sailors at the time. Of course, nowadays we know that the only beer that can cure scurvy is Corona. (Ya with me? Because it comes with a lime. No scurvy jokes? Still too soon?)

No limes in the house? No Coronas? Try dropping a capful of Rose's Lime Juice in your beer. Guys, just don't let your buddy catch you doing it!

It would be years before people realized that scurvy is caused by a vitamin C deficiency and can thus be treated with citrus fruits. Then they started traveling with limes, which is why British sailors, and eventually all Brits, came to be known as "limeys." Too bad for them that Cook wasn't right about the beer . . .

Still, the Kiwis love their beer. Most of the beers consumed in New Zealand are pale lagers. While there is a growing number of smaller brands and microbreweries, the most popular local brands are Export Gold, Monteith's, Speight's, and Tui.

Export Gold is brewed using only New Zealand's "finest malted barley, hops and pure spring water." It's a golden lager of moderate strength that is pleasant and slightly fruity with delicate hop flavors and a crisp, clean finish. Export Gold is called this for a reason—it's won heaps of gold medals.

Like most breweries, **Monteith's** started as a family-run operation. It launched in 1868 and continues to be a popular brand. Similar to Samuel Adams in the United States, they produce several different flavors, and some seasonal and specialty beers as well. In Queenstown, I found that Monteith's is a very popular beer, especially on tap.

Speight's Ale House in Queenstown serves up "southern cooking" and one of the most popular beers in New Zealand. Speight's, founded in 1876 in the city of Dunedin, is known as the Pride of the South, appealing to the down under of the country down under, down under (the people of the southern part, of the southern island, under Australia). It's considered the beer of "hard men" (aka tough guys) on the South Island.

Ironically, after a fire destroyed the Speight's bottling plant in Dunedin on the South Island, they moved their operations to Auckland, on the North Island. (Eh, semantics.)

Tui, named for a New Zealand bird that is shown on the bottle, is an India Pale Ale. As the story goes, in the 1800s beer shipped from England to India (a British colony) was unpasteurized and would therefore undergo a second fermentation in the barrel on the long boat ride. People started to become fans of the "effervescent character" that it gave the beer, and the name "India Pale Ale" stuck. According to the Tui website, their beer is focused on bringing friends together for the "mateship occasion." They say that "mates" getting together like to enjoy a Tui as they "chop some piss, play drinking games and spin a few yarns." Ah, yes . . . chopping piss. Gotta love regionally specific slang!

The Bar, the Bar, the Bar Is on Fire

No, don't go get the extinguisher. Apparently, some New Zealanders like to light things on fire just for fun, or to pay homage to their favorite cocktail bars.

Like just about every other city in the world, Queenstown has a big cocktail scene. There is a bevy of cocktail lounges and upscale bars where one can grab a mixed libation. And one of the most fun places to get a cocktail is the Sky Bar. But stay alert. They have been known to light the entire bar on fire, and then dance on it.

Hangover Plunge

Queenstown is the extreme-sports capital of the world. So after a night dancing on a fiery bar, you can do everything from jetboat up the white-water river and raft down it, or hike up the mountain and mountain-bike down it, to, in their winter (not the same as ours), dropping from a helicopter at the peak of an otherwise inaccessible mountain peak to ski or snowboard down it. While you can find those activities around the world, what you have to do before you leave New Zealand is bungee jump or canyon swing. Queenstown is where both were invented. And nothing takes care of a hangover like an adrenaline rush and the fear of death.

Remedy rating: *Four out of Three Sheets. I chose to do the canyon swing, as-suming (between it and the bungee jump) that it was the lesser of two evils. I was wrong. You start on a platform that juts out 360 feet above the canyon floor. You jump and free-fall two hundred feet before the cable clipped to your harness runs out of slack and swings you out over the canyon. My hang-over was replaced by adrenaline, endorphins, and fear. What really took care of my hangover, though, was doing it a second time, backward . . . And what macho expletive did I blurt out as I plummeted? "Oh, lovely." Real badass, Zane. Reeeeal badass.*

Chapter 13
Japan

Latitude: 36°00' N

Longitude: 138°00' E

What they call it: Nippon

What they speak: Japanese

How to say cheers: *Kanpai!* (To your health!)

Hangover remedy: Ramen, green tea, miso soup, and magic potions

Japan (juh-PAN) 1. A country made of more than four thousand islands. 2. The home of Mount Fuji, an active volcano that has been dormant since 1708, and is the highest point in Japan. 3. A place where it is considered impolite for your hosts to leave your sake glass empty. *Yatta!* (Yay!)

Japan, also known as the House of the Rising Sun, is famous for many things, among them karaoke singers, samurai ninjas, and sake brewers. I wasn't there to murder any perfectly decent songs. And I didn't have time to get into a fight with any mysterious martial arts experts. But I did get to enjoy some remarkable libations. And while Japan does have some notable beers and whiskies, what makes the country a drinking adventure is the sake.

Technically, in Japanese, *sake* can denote any alcoholic beverage. It's similar to how we may use the term *drink*, as in "let's grab a drink," by which you might mean beer or a cocktail. What they call sake, we call a drink. What we call sake, they call *nihonshu*. But, since I'm an American, and I'm writing this book, we'll just call nihonshu "sake," and a drink a drink.

Confused? *Il desu yo* (good). Let's drink some sake.

Number-One Student Make Best for Learning

Typically, the more we understand about how a specific alcohol is made, the more we can appreciate it. Let's face it, vodka isn't "delicious." But learning about the distillation process, the ingredients,

San can be added to first or last names as a form of showing respect. It's similar to adding Mr. or Mrs. to someone's name. Please address me as Lamprey-san, and I'll know you read this book. *Domo arigato* (thank you).

and the history makes it more palatable— even to the point where it's enjoyable. Sake, on the other hand, has the advantage of actually tasting good (to many people).

For my sake education, I headed out of Kyoto to the town of Ono to learn from Nambu-san, owner of the Hanagaki Sake Brewery. I met him at a small and pricey restaurant called Jurakusen.

The Hanagaki Sake Brewery produces high-end sake. Nambu-san was treating me to sushi, a custom that enabled us to know each other and me to earn his respect . . . But drinking rarely happens in Japan without eating. So, after we had consumed about a thousand dollars' worth of food and sake between the two of us, he invited me to his brewery the next morning. Since we had already scheduled this meeting, it was just a formality. But as I was to learn during my time in Japan, formality is a very, very, very important part of getting along with the locals.

For the Sake of Sake

Sake has been made in Japan for centuries, but unlike the French, the Scottish, or the Mexicans, they never thought of making their local specialty Japan-specific in regards to an appellation. Unlike champagne, Scotch, or tequila, which are region-specific, with very clear laws and regulations, sake is more of a free-for-all and can be produced outside Japan. There are sake breweries in China, Southeast Asia, South America, North America, and Australia.

The first sakes were called *kuchikami no,* which translates into "chewed in the mouth." In order to get the fermentation process started, the rice was chewed and then spit into a container. The enzymes in human saliva would begin to convert the starches into sugars. If you're drinking along with a cup of sake in your hands, you probably just put it down. Don't worry, this process hasn't been used for a long time. At least, I hope it hasn't...

Most of the ancient sake breweries were established by wealthy landowners, whose cash crop was rice, a staple of the Japanese diet. They would withhold a portion of rice at the end of the season, which would be sent to their brewery and turned into boozy goodness. Many of those companies are still producing sake today.

At the beginning of the twentieth century, the government got involved in sake. In 1904, the Japanese government opened the sake-brewing institute, endorsing the enamel-coated steel tanks that wouldn't corrode and were resistant to harmful bacteria. More important, unlike the unhygienic older wooden casks, the steel tanks were also resistant to evaporation. Turns out that alcohol can evaporate through wood, and the government wasn't too keen on losing the angel's share (the escaped sake), since they can't tax what evaporates.

Japan's first sake-brewing organization was established in 794, in Kyoto's Imperial Palace.

During World War II, kamikaze pilots ritually drank sake before carrying out their orders. Surprised?

The sake industry changed for good in World War II, when a good portion of the rice that would have been used to make delicious potables was sent off to feed the soldiers fighting in the war. Any rice left over was used to feed the people at home. Thus, there was little left over for luxury items like alcohol. Because of the loss in business, many sake breweries had been shut down by the end of the war. The ones that didn't had a new enemy to face: beer. When Western libations like beer, wine, and spirits started to encroach on sake's territory, less sake was produced than had been for centuries. But thanks to the growing competition, the quality of the sake being produced was improving.

Make Sake

There are four major ingredients in sake. Rice, what lives in your burritos, sushi rolls, and of course, Rice Krispies treats. *Yatta!* Koji, a mold, related to the stuff growing in your shower (I'm not judging, just saying). Water, also known as H_2O, that stuff inside water balloons, pools, or the stuff that falls

In Japan, October 1 is Nihon-shu, National Sake Day in Japan.

from the sky occasionally. And of course, the micoorganisms that make for big hangovers: yeast.

The process, as with any in the world of booze, is simple in concept but intricate in process. You can't just mix rice, mold, water, and yeast and expect to get a delicious beverage. You'd probably get something closer to dough. It's especially complicated to create a beverage that works hot or cold, holds up nicely in cocktails, and can cost as much as five hundred dollars for a bottle (which is how much you'd have to

Dai ginjo is the most premium of premium sakes, made when the sake brewer carefully polishes each tiny little piece of rice down so that it's even tinier, and just a speck remains.

shell out for a taste of Kame no O sake, by Wataribune, a *dai ginjo* sake).

Rice

Sake begins with rice. The first step in getting the whole grain ready to be sakified is to remove the hard outer husk of the rice, leaving only the starchy bit behind, which is what you are used to seeing as "rice." The rice is ground until the protein and oils that make up the outer skin are polished away. The idea is that from removal of the casing, the starches that are left will make a smoother, more delicious, fruitier sake. The general rule is that the more polished the rice, the more premium the sake. These premium sakes are more expensive because it takes a higher volume of the smaller, polished rice to make sake. Oh, and they supposedly taste better.

After the rice is polished, it rests so that it can absorb moisture from the air. The moisture prevents it from cracking when it is immersed in water to re-

Sake rice is harvested in the autumn. The brewing process begins in the winter. The sake is left to mature over the summer, and the batch is usually ready by the following autumn.

Just as the kind of grapes affect the taste of wine, so it is with rice and sake. Sake rice has its own terroir, conditions such as temperature, precipitation, and soil type that affect the quality and taste of the rice. There are about sixty-five different kinds of sake rice. Different strains grow better in different conditions and have different tastes.

move the dust and particles created by the milling process. Then it's cooked by either boiling it or steaming it on a conveyer belt. Once it is steamed, it's separated for different uses; some goes to the vat to wait, while some of the rice is taken to the culture room, where koji mold is added.

Koji

Koji is the mold that is added to the rice to kick-start fermentation. But it's also the name of the rice that's been treated with the koji mold. In a humid room, koji is sprinkled over the rice, which has been spread out on a table. The rice sits for as long as two days, until the right amount of fungus has grown on it.

The koji process can be very regimented, especially at the smaller brewing operations. Some larger sake breweries have automated koji rooms, in which computerized machines distribute the koji mold. But at the Hanagaki brewery, they had a humid, airlocked room with a shirtless man delicately sprinkling koji over a table of rice. We all know how shirts can create a tremendous breeze. Other than the methodical movement of shaking out the mold, he was careful to move very slowly, so as to not upset the still air in the room.

Koji, the helpful little dark green spores scientifically known as *Aspergillus oryzae,* spreads throughout the rice and creates enzymes that break down the starches and convert them into sugars. Without this step, the yeast could not convert the sugars into alcohol. As you know, yeast wants to eat sugar, not starch.

Winemakers don't need to worry about the koji step because there is already plenty of sugar in the grapes for the hungry yeast to devour. Brewers of beer begin with starches that must be converted into sugar before fermentation can begin (the malting process produces the necessary enzymes to feed on the starches and convert them to sugars). Sake makers need a little more help—so koji, the super fungus, comes to the

In less expensive sake, a larger amount of brewer's alcohol may be added to increase the yield of the batch.

Kyoto's Fushimi district is renowned for its sake, often referred to as *onna* (female) sake because of its delicate flavor, which is attributed to the local "medium-hard" spring water.

Seventy percent of the alcoholic beverages consumed in Japan are beer. The remaining 30 percent are sake, *shochu*, wine, and spirits. The most popular spirit is whisky.

rescue and devours those pesky starches, converting them to sugar, so we have ultimately something ideal to drink along with our spicy tuna rolls and to drop into our beers for sake bombs.

Water

Water is an integral member of the sake ingredient family, which is yet another reason why sake shouldn't be referred to as rice wine. (The only guy I ever heard of who used water to make wine was . . . well, you know . . ."Him.") Water is used to clean and steam the rice, as well as during the fermentation process. The kind of water that is used is very important; it's most often spring water. Many sake breweries chose their location for its proximity to natural springs.

Once the koji batch is all "infected" by the mold, it is added to a larger batch to spread. It is after this point that more water and yeast are added to create the alcohol. Then, every day, more steamed rice, koji rice, and water are added to increase the size of the batch.

After it's had time to ferment for several weeks, the entire batch is pressed to extract the liquid. Right before this point, brewer's alco-

Most sake is pasteurized once. This is done by heating it quickly, by passing it through a pipe immersed in hot water. This process kills off bacteria and deactivates enzymes that would likely cause adverse flavor and color later on. Sake that is not pasteurized is called *namazake*, and maintains a certain freshness of flavor, although it must be kept refrigerated to keep it from spoiling.

hol can be added to pull out more of the juice's flavors and aromas. When all of the juices have been extracted, fermentation is halted by filtering and pasteurizing. Then even more water is added, diluting the batch down to around 15 percent alcohol.

Special Designation Make Best for Taste

I visited a sake shop in the Momoyamagoyomae train station to further my sake education. I was practicing saying "Momoyamagoyomae" when I realized that nothing in the shop was in English. It's tough enough walking into a Scotch shop and trying to pick out a suitable bottle of whisky, but this was impossible. Trust me, I was happy to be there. It's just that it was more like being in a museum than a liquor store. While I could appreciate the beauty of the bottles, I had no way of knowing which ones I wanted to purchase and consume. Lucky for me, there was someone on hand to answer my questions and show me the way.

The basic types of sake are *futsū-shu*, "ordinary sake," and *tokutei meishō-shu*, "special designation sake." Futsū-shu

Some sakes, like *teiseihaku-shu*, are made from grains polished to the point that only 20 percent of the rice is left. They're expensive…but come on. You deserve it.

HOW TO MAKE A SAKE BOMB

Warm sake is perfect for sake bombs.

One pint glass filled halfway with beer

One shot glass full of sake

Drop the shot into the beer.

Drink immediately, taking care that the shot glass doesn't slide toward the rim of the glass, smack you in the mouth, and chip a tooth.

is more common and generally less expensive. Tokutei meishō-shu is premium sake; the rice is more polished and it has little or no brewer's alcohol added to it.

The Best Part: Drinking It

Like most alcohol, sake should be stored in a cool, dry, dark place, and it's best kept in a refrigerator. Sake stored at room temperature should be consumed within a few months. It may be served chilled, at room temperature, or heated. Typically, if you order hot sake, in Japan or elsewhere, you'll most likely get low-quality sake, because the heat masks the nuances of the taste.

Aside from being served straight, sake can be used as a mixer for cocktails, such as *tamagozake,* a cocktail made of sake, sugar, and raw egg (sushi eaters will recognize the word *tamago* as the yummy little omelet squares that you can order at Japanese restaurants); saketinis, where sake replaces the vermouth or the gin, depending on your tastes; and the ubiquitous sake bomb.

Sake is usually consumed in small cups, called *ochoko,* like a ceramic shot glass, which you've most likely used if you've ever ordered sake at a restaurant. Traditionally, it may be consumed in a small bowl, called a *sakazuki*, which is common at ceremonies like weddings. Another traditional way of drinking it is from a small wooden box called a *masu*.

Like most premium alcohol, good sake should have a balanced flavor. It shouldn't be overly fruity, dry, or sweet. If you're going to invite friends over to do your own sake tasting, which I highly rec-

Date

When at a sake tasting, it is recommended that you sip, swirl, and spit your sake, as one would do in other booze tastings. But where's the fun in that?! Assuming that you're looking to expand your sake understanding and have some fun with friends, and that you're not doing an official tasting of dozens of sakes for some stuffy event, let the sake go down your throat. There's no reason why your mouth should get to have all of the fun!

ommend, you'll need some palate cleansers for between rounds, or else the tastes will start to run together. Raw, soft tofu is one choice. It's essentially tasteless (like many of my jokes) and you can generally find tofu in any grocery store. There's also the ever-popular salty-sweet jellied jellyfish, which has enough taste to make up for the tofu. You may be lucky enough to find jellied jellyfish in a Japanese specialty store.

Here's a list of some different kinds of sake. Think of it as a cheat sheet for the next time you're ordering a bottle and want to sound knowledgeable about something that is about as confusing to most people as, well, ordering sushi.

Doburoku	Home-brewed (which is illegal in Japan). Lumpy. Made by adding koji to steamed rice.
Fukurozuri	Not mechanically pressed. Hung in bags to let the liquid slowly drip out.
Genshu	Not diluted with water. Higher alcohol percentage.
Koshu	Aged. This one is special, because most sake does not age well.
Muroka	Unfiltered. But not cloudy.
Namazake	Nonpasteurized.
Nigori	Unfiltered. Cloudy. Let the sediment settle and then separate it.
Nigorizake	Cloudy. Contains sediments. Must be shaken before it's poured.
Seishu	Clear. Most common. Color resembles white wine.
Shiboritate	Not allowed to mature for six months, as is traditional for most sakes. Slightly more acidic.
Sparkling sake or crude sake	Carbonated. Unfiltered. A relatively modern type of sake.
Taruzake	Aged in cedarlike wood called cryptomeria.
Teiseihaku-shu	Ultra-premium. Eighty percent of the rice is polished away.

Sake-Drinking Etiquette

1. Never pour your own glass. And when your glass is being poured, hold your glass up off the table with both hands. If you really want to show respect, hold the elbow of the arm holding the glass. This comes from older times, when people wore robes with large sleeves. If you didn't hold the sleeve back, it would get in the way of the pouring.

2. Never let someone else's glass sit empty. If there is an empty glass on the table, it needs to be filled. Many Westerners "complain" that, because their glass is always being filled, they get more intoxicated than they normally would. The trick to avoiding this is to leave your glass half full when you're done drinking, or taking a break. That way it can sit without someone wanting to fill it. I learned this lesson too late.

3. An overflowing glass is a sign of an overflowing friendship. Well, that's what I was told when I overpoured someone's glass in Kyoto. They may have just been trying to make me feel better . . .

> The Japanese word for hangover is *futsukayoi*, which means "two days drunk."

Futsukayoi Cure

You'd think that a culture that applauds drinking to excess would have a long list of hangover remedies—and they do. Here are two of them.

Before make bed sleep. I was advised to stop at a ramen stand on the way home and have a nice big bowl of noodles. The carbs make you nice and full and the salty broth helps you rehydrate.

After make sleep time. Green tea has a nice caffeine kick. Miso soup is salty and comforting. And every convenience store sells rows and rows of magic potions called *genki* drinks, which not only promise to restore you to your regular, slightly less hungover state, but also to cure your cold, give you energy, and raise your sex drive.

Remedy rating: *Two out of Three Sheets. The noodles may have kept my hangover slightly more manageable, but I still woke up feeling like several ronin (rogue samurai) snuck in my room and took turns punching me in the head and stomach. I took the locals' advice and had the green tea, miso soup, and genki drinks. But I'm not sure it left me in better shape. The caffeine cracked me out, the miso left me hungry, and the genki drinks put me over the edge. I was a fidgety mess. My hangover was replaced with ants in my pants. Friendly ants, but ants nonetheless.*

Africa

From characters like Tarzan to character-creators like Ernest Hemingway, from jungle safaris to Masai warriors, Africa's lures and lores have pulled at the curiosity and amazement of Westerners for centuries. I headed to this mysterious continent to drink some backyard brews and some fine wines. Along the way I encountered ostrich eggs, beer made out of honey, beer made out of bananas, wine made out of hibiscus—and liquor made out of winemaking by-products. So here's to the golden plains of Africa, the tribesman who has a plasma TV in the house and a traditional hut behind the house—and the chicken soup for my mouth and for my soul.

Chapter 14
Tanzania

Latitude: 6°00' S

Longitude: 35°00' E

What they call it: Tanzania

What they speak: More than a hundred different languages. The most popular are Swahili and English.

How to say cheers: *Afya!* (Swahili)

Hangover remedy: Chicken soup

Kilimanjaro

Arusha

TANZANIA

Tanzania (tan-zuh-NEE-uh) 1. A country in eastern Africa that borders the Indian Ocean. 2. Home of Mount Kilimanjaro, a dormant volcano that, at 19,340 feet, is Africa's highest point. 3. A place where most things that I drank did not come with a label.

Before you go drinking shots in Tanzania, you're going to need to go to the doctor to get a whole bunch of shots jammed into your arms to make it safe for you to visit. I got twelve. It was worth it, though, because not only were there a lot of animals around (I got a very strange look from a baboon when I was there), but visiting Tanzania was a truly unique experience. If you're looking for culture shock, you'll find it in Tanzania. I sure did. After a few days of throwing back the local booze, I realized that I had yet to imbibe something that had a label on it. Adventurous, sure, but upon reflection, a little bit scary. Still, all those vaccinations offered some measure of protection, right?

Into Africa

My journey began as I exited the giant 747 sitting alone on the runway. It was just after midnight, and as I glanced around I could see nothing but the tiny airport surrounded by darkness. That was my first impression of Africa. There were no lights in any direction, no glow from a city, and no other planes anywhere in sight—even on the tarmac. Most of the passengers deplaned, and as soon as we entered the terminal, our plane made a K-turn, barreled down the runway, and took off into the night, like we were being dropped off from a minivan after soccer practice. That's when I was introduced to Peter Jones, an anthropologist, wildlife conservationist, and safari guide who was

> Unlike other places I've been, where you can bar-hop without worrying about tribal conflicts, poachers, and stampeding elephants, Tanzania is a country best seen with a guide. Most of the country is in the bush, and many of the cities have sections that are best avoided. If you're adventurous, or a seasoned traveler, you could probably do it on your own. I'm both, but I'd still find a recommended local who knows his way around...

dressed like he was taking a break from being Robert Redford's stand-in on the set of *Out of Africa*.

Peter owns an eleven-thousand-acre plot of land called the Ndarkwai Ranch, just southwest of Kilimanjaro. He was going to be my guide through Tanzania.

After crashing at a nearby hotel for the night, we arrived at Peter's "ranch" at noon the next day and threw our stuff in the lavish tents (with wood floors, a bathroom, queen-sized bed, sitting area,

and Internet access). Then we were off to have a drink with some of Peter's neighbors. As we pulled out of the gates I was reminded of the scene in *Jurassic Park* where there were herds of di-

How to tell them you're still thirsty in Swahili: *Nina kiu sana!*

The capital of Tanzania is Dar es Salaam, also known as Bongo to the locals.

nosaurs all milling about together. Right outside Ndarakwai's gates, and a stone's throw from my lavish tent, were baboons, zebras, giraffes, patriot birds, gazelles, and elephants all occupying the same area. A five-minute drive in Peter's open-air Land Rover and we were at his neighbor's house ... well, his neighbor's hut.

Some Masai do leave the tribe for the modern world. As a Masai, your wealth and ultimately your rank in the tribe are determined by the number of cows you own. If you only own a handful, you're better off heading into town and getting a job, because otherwise you're probably not going to get yourself a wife.

Bee Brew

Peter's neighbors are Masai. The Masai are seminomadic cattle herders who live throughout northern Tanzania and neighboring Kenya, and Peter has become friendly with a tribe who live just off his property. On special occasions, which my visit seemed to be, the Masai prepare a batch of bee brew, or *engortorogi,* and have themselves a party.

The largest dung hut in the neighborhood belongs to Swalah, who has seven wives, seven hundred head of cattle, and absolutely no idea how many of the children running about are his. Since Swalah owned all those cows, he was basically the Big Man on Campus. And in my experience, you look to the Big Man to show you the best place to drink.

Bee Brew Basics

Engortorogi is basically mead, a fermented honey brew. It tastes a bit like orange juice that has been left out of the fridge for a few days, but it is really a mixture of water, honey, and aloe roots. The aloe roots are soaked in a honey-water mixture and then left to dry in the sun. Water is heated over a campfire, and then honey is added. In this case, the honey contained chunks of the honeycomb and a slew of dead bees. The Masai dipped the tips of the dried aloe roots into the ashes of the fire and then tossed them in the honey/hot water concoction. It seemed that it might taste like the kind of tea my grandmother would drink, until they added some glowing embers from the fire, covered the pot, took it off the fire, and said that they had to let it sit for four days.

The resourceful Peter had arranged for them to make a batch of bee brew four days before I got there, so I was able to taste it and get a little tipsy with the tribe. There was an acidic bite, but it wasn't too

bad. My guess would be that the alcohol level was around 10 percent (somewhere between beer and wine). As I swatted the flies and threw back more engortorogi, the buzz began to settle in, and Swalah and the others shared the legend of engortorogi with me.

The Legend of Engortorogi

Long ago, a tribesman had been running around on his wife with some other women of the tribe and had picked himself up some nasty gonorrhea. His wife took care of her husband for months, but his condition was just getting worse. He was miserable and so was she. So she set out into the bush to forage for something that would take care of both of their pain: poison.

When she came upon an aloe vera plant, she tasted the sap from its leaves and decided it must be poisonous. But if the leaves were poisonous, she thought, then the roots must be doubly so. So she dug up several aloe vera roots and put them in a pot of boiling water. In order to mask the taste of the poison, she mixed it with fresh honey.

She presented the concoction to her husband and told him it was "medicine" from a shaman. She left it next to his

What do you get when you cross Tanganyika and Zanzibar? The United Republic of Tanzania. Tanzania is a combination of two east African states, which united in 1964.

bed, fully expecting him to be dead by the next day. But the next morning, when she returned to the hut, she found that he was in great spirits, completely cured, and drunk off his gourd.

That's not to say that engortorogi cures the clap. It's just the story I was told.

Alpha Beta Chagga

Later that day, Peter took me thirty minutes from his camp to meet a member of the Chagga tribe. Historically, the Chagga are rivals of the Masai (apparently people don't like it when you raid their cattle and their village). But the rivalry is more memory than current events. Today there is no real bad blood between the two groups. And while many Masai still live as they have for centuries, most of the Chagga converted to Christianity in the last century and are now rooted in the modern world.

Peter introduced me to Baboo. Instead of a BMOC with a hut and a lot of wives, Baboo (a nickname for "grandfather") was an attorney who had a large house, a plasma TV, satellite dish—and a hut in the backyard. He greeted me with a big warm welcome and an enthusiastic two-handed handshake and led me to an area behind his house, where a group of women were singing and making a traditional drink called *mbege*.

Plasma TV aside, in an effort to maintain his heritage on his property, Baboo had re-created a traditional Chagga house made of mud, with a thatched roof. Inside, there was a ready-to-go batch of

Among the Chagga, it's customary for the mbege pourer to drink before handing it to the receiver, to prove that it's not poisonous.

mbege sitting in an open wood barrel. At first glance, it was the most unappetizing cauldron of stuff I'd ever seen (minus anything with dead creatures in it). It had a moist, chunky brown crust floating on top of

According to Chagga custom, the youngest man present serves each guest with a calabash. Since custom also dictates that the server take two drinks from each and every calabash before presenting it to the guest, being the youngest adult at a Chagga mbege party is a good way to get drunk.

it that was occasionally disrupted by a large bubble forcing its way to the surface. Baboo pushed away the crust with a calabash (a traditional ladle fashioned out of a dried gourd) to reveal the mbege liquid. He scooped some up, and before handing it to me, insisted he drink it twice before I taste it.

He drank twice, and then it was my turn. It didn't have FDA approval but it had Baboo's and that was good enough for me. I drank it, and it tasted like an unfiltered Belgian beer with grains floating in it—much better than I expected.

Mmmmmbege!

Baboo brought me back out to the grassy area where the women were, and they gave me a full demonstration of how mbege is made. The main ingredients are bananas and millet, which are prepared

separately and then combined. The bananas are cooked and mashed, then mixed with warm water and hot embers (like the Masai engotorogi). Seven days later, the mixture is strained, leaving a clear, fermented banana syrup. Meanwhile, millet flour has been mixed with water, creating a porridge. The banana syrup is added to the porridge and then allowed to spend the day fermenting.

Just Because They Call It Wine...

Rosella hibiscus leaves (the small reddish leaves underneath the flower) have been used to make tea in Tanzania for years. But in an effort to save food like grapes for eating, locals decided to try to develop alcohol from other sources. So people, including Baboo's wife, make a hibiscus wine, giving an alcoholic twist to hibiscus tea. It's basically a fermentation of millet (like the millet half of the mbege) with the addition of sugar, hibiscus, and yeast.

Since it was presented in a wine bottle and called hibiscus wine, I expected it to taste like wine. But it didn't. It was much sweeter than wine, slightly tangy, with a doughy aftertaste (most likely from the millet). I didn't much care for it. It was too sweet for me. But maybe it was my expectations that were throwing me off. What if, before I drank it, the presenter handed me a glass and said, "First take in the aromatic bouquet. Note the floral overtones and an almost palatable sweetness? Now swirl the glass. You may pick up the scent of freshly baked bread. Now notice undertones of sweetened tea, and some fruity notes. Now taste." But instead, Peter said, "Try this hibiscus wine." I did. And I didn't like it.

Back to Civilization

At this point in my trip, I'd drunk out of a bucket, calabash, and unmarked wine bottle, but I had yet to even have something with a label on it. So I traveled several hours to Arusha, a city with a population of around three hundred thousand. Arusha is a sort of way station for travelers coming to Kilimanjaro. They can stock up on supplies before they hike the mountain, or go on safari. I'm glad to have visited, but I have no plans to ever go back.

Banana Beer

In Arusha, I stopped by Nick's, a bar owned by a guy appropriately named Nick. By day, Nick deals in tanzanite, a bluish-purplish semiprecious stone found in Tanzania. By night he'll pour you a pint of banana beer. Well, that's what he called it. Others call it banana wine. But the label said the product was called Raha and described it as a "Banana Alcoholic Beverage." So who was right?

Banana Alcoholic Beverage is made from ripe bananas, which are softened by being smoked in a pit or hung over a fire. The bananas aren't the sweet, yellow ones you grew up on, but a harsher, starchier, earthier fruit. The cooked bananas are mashed and pressed through a filter; roasted sorghum and water are added to the clear juice that is squeezed out. Then they let the mixture sit for a day before it's ready to be pasteurized and bottled.

I was expecting it to taste like bananas, or at least banana bread. But it tasted like neither. Instead it was like a combination of hard cider and white wine—but cheap hard cider, and inexpensive white wine. At 10 percent alcohol, it packs a punch. And at thirty cents a bottle, with the way it tastes, it's good for one thing—getting Steve McKenna'd.

Konyagi

Nick also busted out a bottle of Konyagi, as well as a small plastic packet of Konyagi, which looked like it should have contained a single serving of ketchup. Konyagi is 35 percent alcohol and is made from sugarcane, but it tastes more like a gin. That's because it's a neutral spirit flavored with juniper berries (and other herbs, flowers and fruits), which is the definition of "gin." The packet was fairly easy to open and got points for pocketability. But opening the bottle came with a ritual. It's something that I've seen done similarly before. Hold the bottle upside down in one hand and smack the bottom of the bottle with the back of your arm. According to Konyagi, this is the duty of the buyer of the bottle. They insist that the bottle cannot be opened if the seal is not broken in this manner. I'll put money on that not being true, and attribute it to tradition, looking cool, and making a fun noise.

Beer

For beer like you're more used to, visit a bar in Arusha called Masai Camp. There you'll find beer, food, and people from just about every continent. As is the case with most countries where the weather is warm year-round, lagers do the job if you're in the mood for something light and crisp. Safari Lager is the strongest at 5.5 percent alcohol. Next down the list is Serengeti Lager, which is around 4.8 percent alcohol. And weighing in at just over 4 percent is Kilimanjaro Lager, the most popular beer in Tanzania.

Another big local favorite is Guinness. You've already heard me talk about how Guinness as a warm weather drink confuses me. This was true in Jamaica, and it was true in Tanzania. Apparently the locals don't agree, because the Guinness I had in Jamaica was bottled in Jamaica, and the Guinness I had in Tanzania was made in Tanzania. I'll never get used to Guinness when the sun shines bright and hot: I'm too programmed into thinking it needs to feel like Ireland outside (chilly) to enjoy one inside. But the Guinness in Tanzania is 7.5 percent alcohol, much stronger than its Irish counterpart. And, like its Jamaican cousin, it was served in a bottle, not on draft, so it wasn't nitrogen-pressurized, either.

A Hangover Remedy Just Like Mom Used to Make

When I'm feeling beat, nothing beats my mom's chicken soup. And who would have thought that in what was quite possibly one of the most adventurous drinking excursions I've ever been on, I'd wind up getting a taste of home when I woke up with a splitting headache?

Down the street from my hotel, on a dirt road bustling with Sunday morning meanderers, was a small restaurant called Sombrero. The owner wasn't Mexican and neither was the cuisine—they just liked the name. When I described my symptoms, they recommended that I have the chicken soup. It was basically half a chicken in a bowl of broth—nothing too exotic, in fact eerily familiar, but a great end to what turned out to be one hell of a drinking safari.

Remedy rating: *Two out of Three Sheets. It did the trick, but wasn't anything out of the ordinary. Chicken soup with a shot of Konyagi may have brought it to Three. But it probably would have also brought up last night's meal . . .*

Chapter 15
South Africa

Latitude: 33°55' S

Longitude: 18°22' E

What they call it: South Africa, Suid-Afrika, etc.

What they speak: English, Afrikaans, Click, and eight other official languages

How to say cheers: Cheers! *Gersondheit! Istulo!* etc....

Hangover remedy: The biggest omelet you've ever seen!

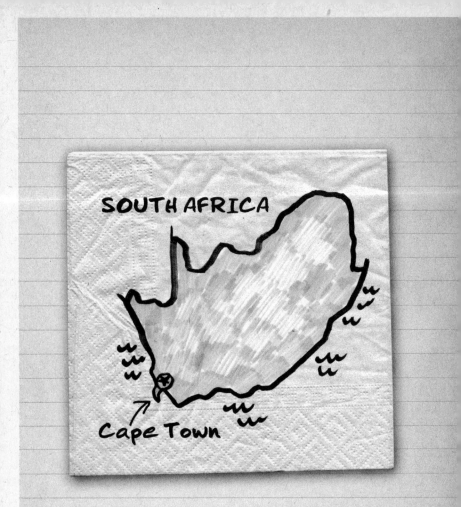

SOUTH AFRICA

Cape Town

South Africa (south-AF-ri-kuh) 1. A country with
eleven official languages. 2. A varied drinking
destination of unparalleled diversity. 3. A place where
the menu can sometimes look like the feeding
schedule at the zoo…

South Africa sits at the very south of Africa. (I know, *duh*.) The so-called Dark Continent is massive; it is the world's second-largest continent, after Asia. But I'd never heard of any African drinks. Do they have any? I thought that I might have to start at the bottom and just drink my way up. Not necessary. South Africa alone con-

tained enough drinking opportunities to require serious hangover remedies, and then some. (I'm lucky I managed to make it to Tanzania. Seriously.) The southernmost country on the African continent will keep you busy. It has a diverse geography, an extremely extensive list of official languages, and residents of many beliefs and drinking customs, many of whom will be

pleased as Pinotage to toss a beverage back with you. So get ready to throw back some cocktails on the beach, kick back with brandy and Cokes at your mate's place, enjoy beer made over a campfire, or sip an excellent local wine at one of the country's many vineyards.

Apartheid, introduced in 1948, was a system of racial segregation in South Africa. In it, black (as well as other nonwhite) South Africans received inferior education, health care, public facilities, job opportunities, and housing. At that time, with black South Africans significantly outnumbering the whites, the only way for the whites to remain in power was to also strip nonwhites of the right to vote.

Don't Stop Wining

South African wines may seem like a new entrant onto the world wine scene. However, they have been producing vino since Dutch settlers introduced winemaking to the region in the 1600s. But trade embargos, brought about by the introduction of apartheid in 1948, severely hampered South Africa's potential to be a major player in the world wine scene. They were prohibited from playing in the global wine game until 1990, when apartheid buggered off. As the markets slowly opened up, South African wines were reintroduced to the world, and they continue to gain in popularity.

With mountainous slopes, coastal breezes, varied elevations, and an endless supply of sun, South Africa has just about every terroir and wine grape known to man. And while the French and Italian varietals flourish throughout South Africa, they also have one varietal that's all their own.

Pinotage

In 1925, Abraham Izak Perold, a professor of viticulture at South Africa's Stellenbosch University, developed a new grape called the Pinotage, which was a hybrid of the pinot noir and Cinsaut grapes. Pinot noir is a tasty red wine grape that is perfectly suited to make, well, pinot noir wine. The Cinsaut, on the other hand, is a sturdy grape that is noted for being good for making, well, nothing. It's most commonly used, in small proportions, in blends of wines. The beauty of the Cinsaut is that it's extremely heat and drought resistant—a feature that comes in handy when growing grapes anywhere in Africa. The drawback is that its toughness also comes across in its flavor.

Some people prefer Pinotage wines (especially the people who make them), but others say it smells of acetone (the stuff in paint thinner and nail polish remover). While I didn't prefer it, I also didn't think it smelled like a beauty salon. I found it to be slightly fruity, but a bit earthy—a strange combination, as wines go. It should be noted that much of the criticism of Pinotage comes from wine connoisseurs in France. And not much pisses off the French wine establishment more than South African winemaker Charles Back.

Goats Do Roam

South Africa's main tourist attraction, as cities go, is Cape Town, which sounds like a place where superheroes live but is actually a stunningly beautiful city that sits in the shadow of the very recognizable, flat-topped Table Mountain. With a climate similar to San Francisco's, Cape Town has proven to be a great place to cultivate world-class wines. Just minutes inland from the city and in just about every direction (except west to the ocean) are some of the world's most desired wine-growing terroirs.

I sat with Charles Back at his Fairview Estate, about an hour outside Cape Town. Charles is a descendant of Lithuanian Jews who came to South Africa in the 1930s, before Hitler's hate-wave could get ahold of them. They bought up an estate near Cape Town originally established by Dutch winemakers in the late 1600s. Today you can visit Fairview Estate, where you may sample any of his various wines. Not only does he own Fairview wines, he makes wines under the labels of Spice Route, Angostinelli, and Goats Do Roam. And it's the Goats Do Roam wines that have the French wine establishment in a huff.

In addition to a wide selection of wines, Charles also has a formidable goat cheese operation. Where the two cross paths is the subject of one of his favorite stories. As it goes, a few years back, his delinquent sons left the gate open on one of the goat enclosures. Instead of eating all the grapes in their path, the escaped goats were very selective and only ate grapes from certain vines. This perplexed Charles, so he sent an assistant out to see which grape varietals they were eating. By "complete coincidence," they ate the exact grapes that are used for making Côtes du Rhône wines. Côtes du Rhône is an official winemaking appellation in France, which means that you can't make a wine using the same recipe and call it Côtes du Rhône unless you make it in that winemaking region, under strict guidelines. So Charles "pays tribute" to his goats' "historic and factual event" by naming his version "Goats Do Roam."

Charles actually entered his version into a Côtes du Rhône wine competition and beat the majority of French entrants. Ever since then, many a French winemaker has claimed that Charles has no right to copy their wines, or to give his wines a name that sounds so similar to "Côtes du Rhône." Charles, on the other hand, stands by his position that "the goats did it." Today his are the top-selling South African wines in the United States and you can find them in many stores in the States. Other wines in the Goats Do Roam line include Bored Doe (sound similar to Bordeaux?) and Goatfather (named for the goat who Charles says protects his secrets). Oh, Charles . . .

Xhosa, also called Click, is one of the official languages of South Africa and is spoken by about 18 percent of the population. The word *Xhosa* actually starts with a clicking sound.

M!ombot!?!?

What better complements an afternoon in the pristine hills sipping French wine knockoffs than an evening in the "township" in the flats, drinking beer from an old paint bucket? Cape Flats is a massive, sprawling shantytown that is home to roughly a million people, although the government admits that it

The exclamation point in *m!ombot* is pronounced as a clicking sound made by creating suction in the roof of your mouth with your tongue. Then, in one motion, snap your jaw downward, letting your tongue pop off the roof of your mouth with a snapping sound: "mmm-snap-ohm-boat."

has no idea how many people actually live there. It's a massive shantytown. As an outsider, it's not recommended that you just wander in and poke around. I ventured out in Cape Flats with armed escorts who had connections to the locals. I never felt threatened. Of course, the escorts took all the credit. When I mentioned how safe I felt, they said, "Yeah, that's because you are with us."

Deep into the maze of streets is a *shebeen* (what they call a bar) that sits miles from any body of water but is called the Waterfront. In these shebeens, you can find a good selection of South African beers, usually sold in forty-ounce bottles to give more bang for the buck. To order one, just go up the bartender, behind the prisonlike steel bars, and slide him your money. I went during the day, before the locals poured in for the night, to try a unique "beer" called *m!ombot,* which is sold in cardboard milk containers or made outside one's home. I sat with Mfundo, who knows the township well enough to take me through the paces of this African original.

M!ombot is an African brew made from a base of cornmeal. It is mixed with sorghum (the grass you learned about in Taipei) and the final product is unfiltered. It looks like thick Yoo-Hoo (a water-based chocolate drink that never seemed to get its props back in the States). M!ombot is made by heating cornmeal and water into a porridge outdoors over an open flame. Mfundo says that it won't work if it's made indoors. When prepared outdoors, naturally occurring yeast can settle into the mixture, triggering fermentation, which converts the sugars into alcohol much as in Lambic beers. They toss in hot coals and allow the mixture to cool and sit outside for a few days, during which the fermentation takes place.

Mfundo told me that his mother makes gallons of m!ombot at Christmastime, when he and his father keep up the tradition of throwing back pints of the stuff, getting Steve McKenna'd and bonding as they reflect over the past year.

Like most alcoholic concoctions, it was an acquired taste. I liked it because of the adoration Mfundo had for it, its social significance, and how intrigued I was at the way in which it's made. But if I had not learned its history from someone who treasured it so, I'd say it tasted like drinking milky beer out of an ashtray. However, if I'd grown up drinking it I'm sure I'd have a different interpretation.

Ijuba (which means "dove" in Zulu) and Chibuku ("The Beer of Africa") are two commercially produced versions of Mfundo's home brew. Packaged in large milk cartons, they taste basically the same as Mfundo's home brew, but without the "campfire" flavor. They're an acquired taste, one that I was not there long enough to acquire. Chibuku is also called Shake Shake because it has a tendency to separate into solids and liquids, so it needs to be shaken before drinking to return it to potable texture. Unlike typical beers, which are clear and filtered, Shake Shake also contains some lumpy bits that you might need broken up before consuming. If you think of it as orange juice with pulp, it's really not bad . . .

HOW TO MAKE A KLIPPY AND COKE

Klipdrift is an 86-proof brandy that, according to the company, "stands for generosity." So pour generously.

Pour Coke into a glass over ice.

Add the desired measure of Klipdrift, and then add a bit more for good measure.

Good Times at the House of Meat

The main drinking scene for tourists in Cape Town is on Long Street, a short strip of road that's home to a good selection of bars and restaurants. Having had years to learn from my mistakes, before hitting the bars I filled my stomach at a restaurant called Kaya Nyama to lay down a foundation for the booze I'd consume later. The name of the restaurant translates into "House of Meat," and believe me, nobody was exaggerating. It would only be slight hyperbole to claim that the walls were actually *made* of meat: They were fully adorned with stuffed heads of the stars of the menu. It was like a gallery of culinary satisfaction, or maybe like the way fast-food joints (and some Chinese restaurants) have pictures of their entrees displayed and backlit above the counters. You could literally order by pointing. Springbok (a type of gazelle), warthog, ostrich, crocodile, and kudo (a large, elklike beast) are all represented. I filled my belly with assorted game as I spoke with Justin, one of the owners, about local drinking customs. As I picked pieces of alligator out of my teeth, he had the bartender bring over a couple of Cape Town's most popular cocktail, a brandy-and-cola combination called "Klippy and Coke." And just for the record, alligator tastes like frog, which tastes like chicken . . .

South Africa is as serious about its brandy as we are about our whiskey. By law, it must be made the same way that brandy is made in the Cognac region of France, which is then called cognac. As we've discussed, the French like to hold tight to their inventions, so only their French counterpart gets to bear the name cognac.

I don't consider large beverage competitions to be the best measuring stick for superior beverages, a statement that will probably revoke my future invitations. I feel like there are too many human variables to be able to crown (or medallion) one winner. However, it should be noted that, since 1999, South Africa has won the "Worldwide Best Brandy" competition more times than any other country.

HOW TO MAKE A SPRINGBOK

This shot is sweet and rich, and more of a gimmick than something you'd ever drink again. If you'd like to try it, the Amarula can be found in many liquor shops across the United States, but the Butler's South African Peppermint Liqueur may be more difficult to find.

Fill a shot glass half full of peppermint liqueur.

Add the Amarula by pouring it over the back of a spoon held just inside the glass. This is done so the two liquids don't mix, giving the shot a two-toned effect.

Still, they use a double-distillation method in copper pot stills and age their brandy in oak barrels for a minimum of three years. South Africans say it tastes just as good, while many French connoisseurs would likely say that it's an inferior product that shouldn't be mentioned in the same breath.

> In the wild, when the fruit from the marula trees becomes overripened, it falls from the tree and begins to rot. Animals such as elephants are reported to have eaten the fallen fruit, which starts to ferment in their stomachs. The animals are said to have been seen intoxicated, stumbling about like Steve McKenna after a bender.

Mixed with cola, Klippy and a three-year-old cognac would be difficult to distinguish because the sugary cola taste competes with the brandy's complexity. K&Cs are popular in Cape Town because they are locally made, and go down easy—maybe too easy.

After my meat feast, Justin brought me to visit two more stuffed creatures mounted behind the bar. This time it was not their heads but rather their asses that were proudly on display. These two unlucky springboks were fitted with spigots that enabled their assholes to pour two South African liqueurs. The first was Butler's South African Peppermint Liqueur. This bright green sweet liqueur is similar to peppermint schnapps in the States. But the other, Amarula, is a bit more unique.

Amarula is a cream liqueur that is made from the fruit of the African marula tree (also known as the elephant tree), which grows wild in southern and western Africa. It's made with the addition of cream and sugar, and has a consistency similar to Baileys Irish Cream. Amarula is the world's second-largest seller of cream liqueurs; the drink is usually served on the rocks.

Getting Witblitzed

Right up the road from Kaya Nyama is Rick's. It's an upscale bar and restaurant where I was welcomed by Billy, the owner, and Ferdinand "Ferdie" Rabie, an ox of a man who owns a local tour company. But more significant to our meeting was that Ferdie won on *Big Brother South Africa* in 2002 and was on record for drinking more than anyone on *Big Brother,* in any country, ever. I was warned that he was a "character." And he didn't disappoint.

Billy and Ferdie introduced me to a liquor called *witblits* (pronounced VIP-litz). Its nickname is "white lightning," and after one taste you'll know why. It was created by the Dutch winemakers who settled in South Africa in the 1600s. Similar to grappa, it's made from distilling the by-products of the winemaking process, such as seeds, stems, and skins. It's been considered moonshine but has recently come to be known as a quality spirit. Many mom-and-pop winemakers make their own version of witblits to follow tradition and to squeeze a little money out of their refuse. Ferdie introduced me to a kind of witblits called Kleinplasie, which is made in the town of Worcester, not far from Cape Town. It is flavored with a wide array of ingredients, such as figs, red bush (a popular South African tea leaf sold in the States as rooibos tea), and chocolate. It actually tastes pretty good.

A fixer, in television and film production, is someone who scouts and coordinates shooting locations. In the case of *Three Sheets,* they often also help with the driving, translating, and sliding into a scene when we need someone who speaks English and knows the local traditions.

But the real witblits, which Ferdie was anxious for me to try, often comes in at around 100 proof. But in this case, the one he busted out was 60 percent alcohol, or 120 proof. Billy pointed out that with this stuff, "You either hate to love it, or love to hate it . . . But it's a killer." After throwing one back, Ferdie wasn't going to leave me alone until I'd done a second shot. It tasted like . . . Well, it tasted like what you'd think it tastes like—really strong booze, because that's what it is. I was done. I had to go see about an oxcart.

The Flaming Oxcart

After sampling South Africa's brews at Mama Africa, another Long Street bar that also serves up plates of exotic meat, I moved on to their signature drink, which I avow to you will never pass my lips again. I bellied up with Harry, the bar's manager, and Peter, our fixer, at the giant bar that's made to look like a fat seventy-foot snake.

Mama Africa's signature drink is called a "flaming oxcart." An oxcart is a wagon pulled by one or more oxen. In this version, it's on fire. So

---

HOW TO MAKE A FLAMING OXCART

Warning: Drink at your own risk. If you do proceed, please drink quickly. If you don't hurry it up, the straw might melt. Also, try not to vomit.

Pour a generous serving of Klipdrift into a margarita glass.

Light it on fire.

Add a springbok (recipe a few pages back) to the flaming mixture.

Suck it up as quickly as you can through a straw while a friend sprinkles cinnamon on the flames, making a sparkling light show.

ALL HAIL SIR SAAZ The Saaz hop is considered a noble hop, which is a designation for four kinds of hops with low bitterness and a good aroma. Hops are like grapes in that where they are grown affects the way they taste. In order to be considered a certain kind of hop, it must be grown in a specific location. The Saaz hop is grown in the Czech Republic, and Hansa imports it for their pilsner. Words used to describe its flavor include *spicy, cinnamony, earthy.* Tell me again when the taste of earth (dirt) started sounding delicious?

is the drink. I almost threw up while I was drinking it, thanks to the cinnamon light show. My pal Peter tried not to vomit, and instead he threw up his drink through his nose. It was disgusting and something I had never seen the likes of—and hope I never do again. Still, it was remarkable enough to be worth mentioning. From now on, if that ever happens again, I shall be amazed, and will say that that person "Petered."

South Africa's Top Three Brews

Castle Lager: The country's top-selling beer is Castle Lager, a 5 percent alcohol pale lager that's advertised as "somewhat dry, somewhat bitter, never sweet." I concur. Castle Brewery was founded in 1894 by Charles Glass, who originally came from England to South Africa during its gold rush. When his prospecting didn't "pan out" (that's where that expression comes from), he turned to gold of a different kind: beer. He used his fellow miners as test subjects for his various brews, until he locked down a recipe in 1884. Eleven years later, in 1895, when SAB (South African Breweries) was formed, he made his fortune, cashed out, and returned to England, leaving behind a brew that has stood the test of time. Today the Castle brand also puts out a Castle Lite and a Castle Milk Stout.

Hansa Lager: SAB/Miller now technically owns and produces many of the popular beers in South Africa, including Hansa, which makes a fairly nondescript lager with a similar alcohol content to Castle; they first launched their pilsner in 1975. Their slogan is "The Kiss of the Saaz Hop."

Since my visit, South African Breweries has merged with Miller to become the largest maker of beer on the planet. Not only do they make a lot of beers you're familiar with, they also make the stuff you can drink from cardboard cartons in Cape Flats. In other words, you cannot escape the broad beer-making reach of SAB/Miller.

Black Label: Black Label, another often-hoisted beer in South Africa, is also now technically owned by SAB/Miller. In South Africa, the local name for Black Label is Zamalek, which is also the name of a soccer team—from Egypt. As the story goes, some years back an Egyptian soccer team called Zamalek beat the pants off a South African team. The team's logo was written in a font similar to the Black Label logo. The word *zamalek* means "strong one" in Egyptian, and since Black Label is 5.5 percent alcohol—slightly stronger than most other South African lagers—the beer came to be known in South Africa as Zamalek. However, in Egypt, where the word comes from, Zamalek remains the name of a soccer team and has nothing to do with beer.

The Biggest Hangover Helper You've Ever Seen

If you believe that a big meal is a great remedy for a hangover, then the perfect breakfast awaits you at the Westcoast Ostrich Ranch, where Gavin Kanigowski and his son, Pawel, have been raising ostriches for the tourist business, leather, meat, and eggs. After just a twenty-minute drive from Cape Town's Waterfront (the real Waterfront, not the bar in Cape Flats), you can share in the biggest omelet you've ever seen, made from the biggest eggs you'll ever see, with a great view of Table Mountain.

- One ostrich egg is equivalent to twenty-four regular-sized chicken eggs and contains about two thousand calories.
- The eggs are about 5.9 inches long and weigh just over three pounds.
- A two-hundred-pound man (me at the time) could stand on two eggs (one foot on each egg) without breaking them (they're that big, and that tough). A full-grown ostrich can stand nine feet tall and weigh up to 330 pounds, so my fat ass was nothing.

HOW TO COOK AN OSTRICH EGG

Before they can cook your eggs at Westcoast Ostrich Ranch, they must first get the egg out of the shell. Ostrich eggs are so hard that some people actually use power drills to drive a hole through the shell. But before you get out your toolbox, note that at Westcoast they do it the old-fashioned way: with a spoon and some manpower.

Use the back of a spoon to tap the tip of your ostrich egg until you break on through.

Stick a straw in the resultant hole, and blow on it until the pressure forces the egg out of the shell through the same hole and into a bowl. Whip with a big fork until mixed.

Empty the contents of the bowl into a giant frying pan.

Cook until it looks like scrambled eggs.

Remedy rating: *Two out of Three Sheets. But because there is just so much egg in an ostrich egg, it's too thick in the pan to congeal like a typical scrambled egg. So the consistency of the scramble at Westcoast was more like porridge than your typical brunch fare. It was rich, it tasted like eggs, and it was an experience I'll treasure, but I still wouldn't fight an ostrich just for the privilege of cooking one of their progeny.*

Conclusion

When I started hosting *Three Sheets*, I saw it as nothing more than a job. Sure, I jumped in with both feet, and willingly so. But had I landed a gig hosting a show about home improvement, cars, music, or nudists, I would have just as easily become an expert in those fields (although it should be noted that despite my lack of training, I am an excellent nudist). As it was, after spending several years traveling the globe and drinking enough to fill a pool (one big enough for a diving board), I have become an accidental expert.

That's not to say that I knew nothing about booze before I started *Three Sheets*. I went to a four-year college for five years. If you believe that it's because I "switched my major so many times," then I'll sell you my shares in the Brooklyn Bridge—I'll let you have them for a steal!

The World

In my travels, I've learned a great deal more than how to throw back drinks with the locals. I've learned that people across the world are not that different. We need to love and to be loved, and we know the importance of family and friends. However, until we've found a way to speak for ourselves, instead of having elected (or appointed) officials do it for us, there will always be lingering political agendas. Unfortunately, I have witnessed lands affected by this—lands ravaged by conflict and war, some with wounds that have yet to heal. If it were up to me, I'd gather the politicians in a pub and tell them that they were not leaving until they had finally worked it all out.

My Favorite Drink

One of the most frequent questions that I'm asked, aside from "Do you need an assistant to travel with you?," is "What's your favorite drink?" That would be like asking me to pick a favorite sibling. Okay, maybe that's easier: my sister. But it's close!

The truth, and it may sound like a politician's answer, is that my favorite drink is most often the one that I'm drinking. Makers of alcohol are incredibly passionate about their products. To them the drink is not just a collection of ingredients or something to get drunk from; it's tradition, heritage, and their livelihood. Their recipes have either been passed down for generations or are new concoctions that have yet to catch on. Regardless, everything I've consumed is extremely important to someone somewhere. If you're astute, you can taste the blood, sweat, and tears. But don't worry, they're usually killed off by the alcohol.

So when someone asks me to pick a favorite drink, I stand there frozen, racking my brain. I don't have a short answer for that question.

As I sat in Poland at a makeshift table by a lake in the middle of the woods with the creator of Chopin vodka and had him explain the significance of vodka to his country and the importance of each of its ingredients, I didn't feel like a beer. I felt like Chopin vodka. When I was in the four-hundred-year-old Kings Head pub in Galway, Ireland, with the town's honorary mayor, listening to him regale me with stories of the most popular beer in Ireland (and the world), I salivated for a Guinness. And as I stood in a sheep-shearing hut outside of Queenstown, New Zealand, listening to Malcom Willmott tell me the history of Hokonui, there was nothing else that I wanted in my cup.

As for when I'm home . . . Well, since I get paid to drink, it has become less of a leisure-time activity. So while I have a nicely stocked bar with booze from a hundred countries, I usually go for a beer. When I go out on the town, however, I'll scan the liquor shelf behind the bar to see if there is something that can transport me to some other destination around the world.

I hope that this book has called up memories of a foreign place that you've been to, or, even better, inspired you to take a trip to a far-off land. At the least, I hope that I've encouraged you to try something new. Cheers! *Kanpai! Skål! Istulo! I Sveikata! Salud! Gan bei! Prost! A votre santé! Okole maluna! Gezondheid! Sláinte! Zum Wohl! Na zdrowie! Afya! Choc-tee! Mabuhay! Sláinte bráden, bod mór, agus bás in Eireann!*

Acknowledgments

As wonderful as my job is, it has not come without sacrifices. As much as I have fallen in love with the places I've been, there truly is no place like home. As I sat alone in a plethora of hotel rooms, I missed my family. With all of the far-off places I have visited and amazing things I've experienced, nothing can compare to the feeling I get when my son sees me and his eyes light up. This book is for you.

I also know that, without the amazing *Three Sheets* team that I am a part of, I could easily look like an ass. My heartfelt thanks goes to Mike "Big Daddy" Kelly, Christina "I'll Drink That" Kindwall, Curtiss "Miss Thang" Marlowe, and Eric "The Sound Monkey" Soma (it's in alphabetical order, Eric). Okay, fine! I'll thank Bert "Heavy Jaw" Klasey too! I would also like to thank Steve McKenna, Jim "The Cop" Reisinger, and Pleepleus for their comic relief. I'd also like to thank the editors and researchers for making me look smart. Thank you, Sandra Bark, for your tutelage and hard work. And I don't want to forget the little people; Matt Chan, Ryan Doherty, Ivo Fischer, Jodi Flynn, Karen Marines, Emilio Nuñez, Rebecca Oliver, and Chad Youngblood.

And, most certainly, the show (and therefore I) would be nothing without the incredible legion of fans who appreciate what we do. THANK YOU!

Zane Lamprey, a native of Syracuse, New York, has resided in the Los Angeles area since the end of the last century. In addition to hosting *Three Sheets,* Zane has also hosted the series *Have Fork, Will Travel* on the Food Network, where he visited different countries and ate. With his unique ability to present relative information in a comedic and entertaining format, he was just as successful at getting people to open up over fish stew as he was with a sake bomb. When he's not engaged in television and film ventures, writing more books, or traveling the globe, Zane can usually be found doing his stand-up somewhere around the country. For up-to-date info, visit ZaneLamprey.com.